PILOTING WITH CONFIDENCE

CHARTS, CHECKLISTS, SYSTEMS & COCKPIT TIPS

D1602812

WARNING

The purpose and intent of this book is to give the reader the benefit of the author's experience of over 30 years of flying general aviation aircraft. It is not intended to teach airmanship of piloting technique. THIS BOOK IS NOT A SUBSTITUTE FOR OFFICIAL SOURCE MATERIAL APPLICABLE TO THE READER'S SPECIFIC FLIGHT, FLIGHT OPERATION AND AIRCRAFT AS PROVIDED BY THE FEDERAL AVIATION REGULATIONS, FEDERAL AVIATION AGENCY, THE AIRCRAFT MANUFACTURER'S RECOMMENDATIONS AND THE PILOT OPERATING HANDBOOK. SHOULD THE INFORMATION CONTAINED IN THIS BOOK DIFFER IN ANY WAY FROM THESE OFFICIAL SOURCES OF INFORMATION, IT SHOULD BE DISREGARDED IN FAVOR OF THOSE OTHER SOURCES. FAILURE TO RELY ON OFFICIAL SOURCE MATERIALS MAY RESULT IN SERIOUS PERSONAL INJURY OR DEATH.

Because the aviation environment is constantly changing, as is technology's role in aviation, the reader must take responsibility for acquiring all the information applicable to his or her specific aircraft, as well as all government initiated rules, regulations and directives applicable to the specific flight operation he or she is conducting. Since this information is constantly changing, the reader must keep abreast of all new information applicable to his or her flight and related operation and the latest information should be relied upon rather than the information contained herein.

PILOTING WITH CONFIDENCE

CHARTS, CHECKLISTS, SYSTEMS & COCKPIT TIPS

First Edition

James Spudich

Piloting with Confidence - Charts, Checklists, Systems & Cockpit Tips
Copyright © 2004 by James Spudich

Published by AJ Publications, LLC
P.O. Box 7435
Menlo Park, California 94026
http://www.ajpublicationsca.com

Printed in the United States of America

First Printing, First Edition, July 2004

ISBN 0-9748117-0-X

To Mike Nash, my first instructor who took me through my private pilot certificate and beyond and taught me the meaning of feeling one with the airplane, and to Avram Goldstein, who trained me in precision instrument flying and emphasized the importance of making my own checklists.

Thank you for purchasing this book. While it has been carefully proofread, mistakes undoubtedly have been missed. Any corrections that you may have, no matter how small, would be greatly appreciated. They can be emailed to ajpublic@ajpublicationsca.com, or mailed to AJ Publications, LLC, P.O. Box 7435, Menlo Park, California 94026.

Contents

Illustrations

Preface

Organization in the cockpit is essential to safe flying. A good pilot is never finished improving his or her organizational skills. The point of this book is to instill into young pilots' minds the importance of generating their own charts, checklists and other helpful aids that reflect their own personal needs and habits. Examples of such charts, checklists and cockpit tips that I have generated for myself over the last thirty years of flying are illustrated in this book.

I find the charts and checklists that I describe invaluable for every flight that I take. I love flying in the West, and scattered throughout the book are selected photographs from various trips. These are a reminder of how spectacular and magical flying can be.

While a major point of this book is to stimulate you to create your personal charts and checklists, you may find mine useful as basic templates. The more you indulge in this activity, the more confidence you will have as a pilot and the safer you will be. And the safer you are, the happier you and your passengers will be.

In the process of creating checklists, you should constantly be asking why you are checking the things that you do. That is, be sure that you understand the airplane systems. The second chapter emphasizes this and gives brief descriptions of a variety of systems in your airplane. Understanding the systems makes you a safer pilot.

Additional chapters include methods for easily checking your weight and balance before every flight, getting started with the use of GPS equipment, and mastering and remembering the diverse rules and regulations associated with flying. Making use of your computer and personal digital assistant (PDA) is emphasized throughout the book.

Keep the skies safe and enjoy the magic of flying!

Acknowledgments

This book owes its existence in a fundamental way to my wife Anna, who encouraged me one summer day in 1975 to take flying lessons out of Friday Harbor Airport, in between experiments that she and I were carrying out on cell division of fertilized sea urchin eggs at the Friday Harbor Marine Biology Laboratories. She only asked that I do whatever it takes to be extra careful. I thank Avram Goldstein for encouraging me to write this book, Dominique Marais, Suzanne Pfeffer, and Channing Robertson for editing an early draft and offering useful suggestions, and John Mercer and Uta Francke for sharing with me some of their great photographs taken from the cockpit of small planes, which are intermingled with my own throughout the book.

Photo by James Spudich

The serenity of flying in calm conditions between layers is an unforgettable experience

Chapter 1
Create Your Personal Written Checklist

My thirty years of flying have taught me the importance of creating my own charts and checklists to use in flight. How many times have you searched for the written preflight checklist that is supposed to be in your rental plane? With more experience, you also have discovered that such checklists are minimal and not necessarily organized in a fashion that suits you. In the absence of finding it, you may have even been willing to lapse into using the acronym CIGAR and forego the written checklist completely. This may take care of some of the essentials, such as Carb heat and Cowl flaps-Instruments-Gas-Attitude (trim)-Radio, but do not expect to get away with this for very long without getting yourself into a compromising situation.

Flying is a wonderful and personal experience. You owe it to yourself to personalize written information that you have with you while sauntering along the Pacific Coast at sunset, flying to your favorite airport for an evening dinner with a friend, taking a flying weekend fishing trip to Montana, or simply doing pattern work at your home airport.

Chapter 2 deals with additional charts and checklists, but let's start with creation of your basic personal checklist that will aid you in checking your airplane before takeoff as well as in all phases of flight, including shutdown and tiedown upon reaching your destination.

Create Your Personal Checklist

Create a personal checklist for each airplane that you fly. Each of mine is two-sided and measures 5 x 8.5 inches, which fits neatly into one Jeppesen or ASA 7-ring sheet protector, as do most of the charts and diagrams that I describe in this book. I fly the Piper Dakota a lot, and I use that as an example here (Fig. 1A and B).

Figure 1A has information relevant to before starting through cruise, and Figure 1B deals with descent through shutdown, with extra space used for short field information. Each major block is divided into subgroups (separated by underlines).

Under **BEFORE START**, Figure 1A, the first thing I do is make sure that external preflight is complete. Issues often overlooked are making sure there is no tow bar left in the nosewheel and that the airplane is completely untied. Then I check that all required documents are on board (when did you last check that?), that the avionics master and all relevant switches are off, that the circuit breakers are in, and that lights are as required.

My next subgroup is to check trims, fuel selector, flaps, and carb heat (*notice they are all near one another in the cockpit*). Next I brief my passengers, make sure all seats are locked and seat belts are secure, and make sure the cabin door is locked (a logical subgroup, right?).

ENGINE START is self explanatory.

BEFORE TAXI includes getting the ATIS and setting the altimeter and directional gyro (DG). While I **TAXI** and I'm sure that I'm clear of crowded areas, I check my brakes, make sure my

PIPER DAKOTA PA-28-236/G

BEFORE START		TAXI	
Preflight (Documents)	complete	Brakes	check
Avion Mstr/ All Switches	off	MC, AI, DG, TC, VSI	check
Circuit Breakers	in	Takeoff Briefing	complete
Lights (check)	as reqd	**BEFORE TAKEOFF**	
Trims	set for T/O	Flight Controls	correct
Fuel Selector (check)	fullest tank	Mixture	rich
Flaps	up	Throttle	2000 rpm
Carb Heat	off	*Magnetos (175dp,50Δ)	check
Passenger Brief	complete	*Prop (RPM,OilP,ManP)	cycle 3x
Seats	locked	*Carb Heat (100dp)	check, cold
Seatbelts	secure	*Engine Gauges	check
Cabin Door	locked	*Ammeter & Alternator	check
ENGINE START		*Vacuum (4-6")/Alt Stat	check both
Mixture/Prop	full forward	Throttle	900 rpm
Throttle (cold/pump 1x)	1/4 " open	Fuel Selector, Aux Pump	fullest, on
Carb Heat	cold	Trim	aft neutral
Primer	5c/2h/lock	Transponder	Alt, 1200
Aux Fuel Pump	on	Annunciator Panel	set
Propeller Area	clear	Flight Instruments	set, check
Battery Master	on	Primer	in, locked
Alternator Switch	on	Lights	as reqd
Beacon lights	on	Doors, Windows, Belts	secure
Starter	engage	Autopilot	off
Throttle	900 rpm	Time Off	note
Engine Instruments	check	**NORMAL TAKEOFF** Best Glide 85	
Oil Press	green	Flaps	up
Aux Fuel Pump	off	Rotate	65 KIAS
BEFORE TAXI		Climb Out	80 KIAS
Mixture	lean	500' (MP, RPM)	25, 2400
Transponder 1200	standby	1000' (Fuel Pump,Ldg Lt)	both off
Radio Master	on	**CRUISE** 140 KIAS	
Avionics	set / check	Cruise Power	24, 2400
ATIS	copy	Landing Lights	off
Altimeter	set	Mixture	lean
DG	set	Gauges	check
Flight Instruments	check	**CRUISE CLIMB** 100 KIAS	
Fuel Selector	fullest tank	Power	25/ 2400
		Mixture	rich/ as reqd

Fig. 1A. Checklist for All Phases of Flight — front side
(Not to be used without verification of information from official sources)

magnetic compass (MC), directional gyro (DG), and turn coordinator (TC) are moving appropriately, and that my attitude indicator (AI) is not moving and my vertical speed indicator (VSI) is at zero.

I am now at the run-up area and ready for **BEFORE TAKEOFF**. The first thing I check is flight controls. I check full range of motion of the yoke and make sure that the various movements of the yoke are properly reflected in the movements of the aileron and elevator. This check is especially critical after maintenance, either 100-hour or annual maintenance, because cables may have been reattached incorrectly or simply not reconnected at all.

The next subgroup has all the checks using the throttle at 2000 rpm. These are checking the magnetos, cycling the props, and checking the carb heat, engine gauges, ammeter and alternator, vacuum, and alternate static port. The throttle is then reset to idle at 900 rpm.

The next subgroup is fuel, trim, mixture, transponder, and annunciator panel (yes, *all in the same general location in the cockpit*).

The final subgroup before takeoff is to check flight instruments, primer, lights, doors, windows, seat belts, autopilot, and noting the time of takeoff.

NORMAL TAKEOFF (best glide for the plane is noted here, considering its importance) is self explanatory, as is **CRUISE** and **CRUISE CLIMB**. But one point to remember is to check your floating compass when aligned on the runway for takeoff. This is an excellent time to check that it is giving the appropriate reading.

Now I'm ready for the second side of the checklist (flip side of the 7-ring sheet protector) (Fig. 1B). Note across the top important information about the airplane (useable fuel 72 gal, 4.9 hr fuel with 45' reserve, 235 HP@2400 RPM, 6 cylinder air-cooled engine).

Useable Fuel 72 gal, 4.9 h _w_ 45' res, 235 HP@2400, 6 cyl air

DESCENT			AFTER LANDING	
Fuel Selector	fullest tank		Flaps	up
Mixture	incr as reqd		Trims	set for T/O
Descent Power	set		Mixture	lean
Avionics	set		Carb Heat	off
ATIS	copy		Transponder	standby
Altimeter	set		Lights	as reqd
Lights	on		Fuel Pump	off
Engine Instruments	check		**SHUTDOWN**	
Flight Instruments	check		Avionics Mstr, Electrical	off (-beacon)
Approach Briefing	complete		Throttle	900 rpm
APPROACH			Mixture	Idle Cut-Off
Landing Light	on		Beacon at key removal	off
Fuel (Selector, Pump)	fullest, on		Magnetos, key	off, out
BEFORE LANDING (on downwind)			Master	off
C- Carb Ht	off/ as reqd		Control Lock	secure
G- Fuel Selector, Pump	fullest, on		Log	time
U- Undercarriage	dn, lkd, gn		Covers (windws,nose,pt)	install
M- Mixture	rich		Postflight Inspection	clean up
P- Props/ Primer	full fwd, lkd		Doors	lock
S- Seat Belts	on		Tie Downs	secure
NORMAL LANDING	**72 KIAS**		**SHORT FIELD TAKEOFF**	
Downwind (MP, Flaps)	20, 0°		Flaps (2nd notch)	25°
Abeam (MP, Flaps)	15, 10°		Max usable rwy/ Brakes	hold
Base Flaps as Reqd	80 KIAS		Throttle	full forward
Final Flaps 40°	72 KIAS		Brakes	release
Short Final G-dlg, Prp-ff	72 KIAS		Elevator Control	tail-low attit
Landing	72 KIAS		Rotate	50-60 KIAS
GO-AROUND			Climb Out	73 KIAS
Throttle	full forward		50-ft Obstacle Cleared	85 KIAS
Flaps	to 25°		**SHORT FIELD LANDING**	**60 KIAS**
Undercarriage	up		Downwind (MP, Flaps)	20, 0°
Pitch	75, then 85		Abeam (MP, Flaps)	15, 10°
Flaps @ +VSI, Vy	retract		Base Flaps as reqd	80 KIAS
			Final full flps G-dlg,Prp-ff	65 KIAS
			Shalw apch unless obs	65 KIAS
			Power	some
			Landing	50-65 KIAS
			At Tchdwn	pwr off, flps up, brakes

Fig. 1B. Checklist for All Phases of Flight — back side
(Not to be used without verification of information from official sources)

Getting ready for the **DESCENT**, I always check first that my fuel selector is on fullest tank – changing tanks should be done at the highest altitude (but I do pay attention to terrain – engine failure upon changing tanks is not unheard of). After taking care of fuel, mixture and descent power, I'm ready for the next subgroup. I set the avionics, check the ATIS, and set the altimeter. This takes me to the third subgroup – lights, engine and flight instruments, and approach briefing for the passengers.

Now I'm ready for the **APPROACH**, which is self explanatory. My **BEFORE LANDING** check always includes checking undercarriage is down, locked and green *even in airplanes with fixed gear*. By assuming that I am always flying a retractable gear airplane, it is less likely that I will forget to put the gear down when I do fly a retractable.

NORMAL LANDING includes a note showing the normal landing airspeed, an important number to nail on final for the best landing possible. On short final, I *always* check and say out loud "gear down locked and green" (or "gear down locked and no green showing because this is a fixed gear airplane") and "props full forward." You will greatly diminish the probability of a belly up landing in a retractable gear airplane if this habit is ingrained deeply enough into your routine short final approach procedure. Remember on the **GO-AROUND** that you only retract *partial* flaps until you have positive vertical speed indication and have achieved Vy.

AFTER LANDING and **SHUTDOWN** are straightforward, but sometimes I preflight an airplane in the club that I belong to and find no control lock installed, or no covers on the windows, or the airplane unlocked. So do *check your written checklist* before leaving the site of the airplane. If you are flying an airplane with cowl flaps, open them after landing while you taxi to allow engine cooling, and then close them at shutdown to prevent birds or other items from getting into the engine compartment.

Since a **SHORT FIELD TAKEOFF** or **SHORT FIELD LANDING** may be desired on the spur of the moment, I include those procedures here. Upon touching down on a short field landing, the minimum landing distance will be realized if you immediately go to power off, flaps up, brakes on – many pilots skip the flaps up due to the danger of raising one's gear by mistake when flying a retractable gear airplane. The most important part of the short field landing is setting it up properly – if all is correct on final, you are pretty much set. This means you have stabilized the approach as soon as possible and have the recommended airspeed.

Make a personal checklist that will aid you in checking your airplane before takeoff as well as in all phases of flight

Photo by James Spudich

When you observe the landscape for the first time from a small plane, your perspective of the world is altered forever

Chapter 2
About Systems and the Purposes of Your Checklist Items

In the first chapter I emphasized the importance of creating your personal checklist, but why do you check what you do? How are the systems you are checking supposed to work, and what failures are you likely to catch by using your checklist during the various phases of flight?

This section examines each item of the checklist described in Figures 1A and B, and discusses the underlying systems and instruments that come into play. The logic behind each of the checks is discussed.

BEFORE START

PREFLIGHT (DOCUMENTS) - complete

Your preflight of the airplane should include every part of the airplane accessible to you. The goal is to be sure that all is secure before you start the engine. The external preflight deserves adequate time for a thorough inspection. Do not simply check that all is basically functioning, but be aware that all of the parts of your plane have a definite lifetime. Look for signs of wear and tear. A crack in the structural part of the skin is reason to ground the airplane. In my thirty years of flying, I once gave an inadequate look at the main gear assembly on my Piper Comanche and failed to notice that the left gear pin was about to give. Well, it gave on takeoff and I was lucky that the gear didn't slip out of its socket, which is possible in that airplane under those circumstances. I landed gently and safely, but it didn't have to turn out that way. Never be in a hurry. That's the time something will be wrong and you'll miss it.

On your exterior preflight check, besides the obvious, do not forget to check that:

√   your cooling air pathway and your engine air intake pathway are completely open

√   your oil grade is correct for the season - in general, SAE 50 for surface temperatures above 40°F and SAE 30 for colder temperatures

√   the color of your gas is correct - the correct octane is important for your particular engine

√   your tires have plenty of tread and are properly inflated - tires are often neglected in preflight, but a blowout on takeoff or landing can lead to loss of control more than you imagine, and the results can be disastrous.

Part of your preflight is that your required documents are on board. Remember AROW? Airworthiness certificate, Registration certificate, Operations manual/placards, and Weight and balance data. Check that these are in your airplane before starting the engine. In a brand new airplane, the FAA certifies the airplane under the specifications listed in the Type Certificate Data Sheets (TCDS). Thus, an Airplane Flight Manual is created that is specific to that very airplane. When the airplane is altered from the original TCDS, the change must be approved by the FAA in a Supplemental Type Certificate (STC). Modifications also occur due to an Airworthiness Directive (AD). Compliance with and adherence to TCDS's, STC's and AD's are required for your aircraft to be airworthy. In addition, all parts used to meet the compliance requirements must be approved by the FAA. If not, the airplane's airworthiness certificate becomes invalid.

   Speaking of weight and balance, do not load up your airplane with full passengers without carrying out a weight and balance check! Ideally, you should check weight and balance every time you fly. I describe easy ways to do this in Chapter 5. Follow my suggestions and you can do your weight and balance check painlessly and in less than 60 seconds.

   One item often overlooked in the preflight is a check of the emergency locator transmitter (ELT). The FAA requires that you have an operating ELT in the airplane. The ELT has a vibration sensor switch, which is turned on in the event of experiencing a G load in excess of the permissible range (>5 G's). Thus, if you have an accident, the ELT is activated and transmits a signal on 121.5 MHz. One thing that you have to be mindful of is that slamming the baggage door or having a particularly hard landing can activate your ELT. To check for inadvertent activation, tune in on 121.5 and see if you are receiving an ELT signal. Manually flipping the ELT switch on and tuning in to 121.5 is also the way to check that your ELT is functioning. But remember to turn it off again!

AVIONICS MASTER/ ALL SWITCHES - off

   Upon preparing for engine start, all avionics should be off to protect them from sudden power surges during engine startup that can damage the avionics equipment. One thing to remember is to keep your battery in the circuit even after engine start, because it acts like a buffer against spikes in voltage, and therefore protects your electrical system (see below for more on your electrical system).

CIRCUIT BREAKERS - in

   The circuit breakers are one type of protection of the electrical circuits. They are better than replaceable fuses since they can simply be reset after about a 2-minute cool down period. An element in the circuit breaker expands if it becomes overheated and the circuit breaker trips, opening the circuit.

What is the logical thing to do if a circuit breaker pops in flight? This can happen due to some momentary glitch in the system, and does not mean that anything is necessarily wrong with the instrument in question. Thus, the thing to do is to turn off the instrument in question, wait for 2 minutes for the circuit breaker to cool, push in the breaker to reset it, then turn the instrument back on. If the breaker pops again, then leave it out and turn the instrument off.

LIGHTS (CHECK) - as required

Minimally, you need to have position lights and anticollision lights on. Position lights are red on the left wing tip, green on the right wing tip, and white on the tail. Remember the rule "red on right, watch out!" This means a plane is coming directly toward you.

The anticollision light is either the common rotating red beacon or strobatic lights. Often your plane will have both. The high intensity strobe lights should be turned off while taxiing before takeoff or after landing. They can be blinding to other pilots operating near you, and can give airplanes in flight or on approach the illusion that you are on the runway, having just landed or getting ready to take off.

Why didn't I mention landing lights? Because they are not required for VFR flight during either day or night. Landing lights are notorious for burning out before you are on final approach. This means, of course, that you need to keep up your practice of night landings without your landing lights on. It's also good practice to learn to taxi around with no taxi lights or landing lights. They both can burn out in flight, and with no experience, it can be unnerving to try to navigate on the airport.

TRIMS - set for takeoff

Once, I landed at Santa Barbara airport and shut down the airplane. After a long day, I preflighted the plane and began my takeoff roll at night. For some reason, the plane was hugging the runway even though my takeoff speed had already been reached. I was an inexperienced pilot and this was somewhat unnerving, since I had not experienced this before. Once I realized that I had forgotten to set the trim tab for takeoff (it was trimmed forward for the landing), I quickly trimmed back and off I flew. Thankfully, Santa Barbara airport has a long runway. I have never forgotten the trim setting after that and also added resetting the trim for takeoff as an important item of my after landing checklist.

FUEL SELECTOR (CHECK) - fullest tank

Fuel starvation is the cause of so many unnecessary accidents. This check appears multiple times on my checklist.

FLAPS - up

You lowered your wing flaps to thoroughly check them during your external preflight. It is considered bad form to taxi out to the runway with your flaps down, and you certainly don't want to try a takeoff with full flaps. The drag may mean that you don't leave the runway before you run out of it! This is the time in your checklist to make sure they are up.

Another important category of flap is the cowl flaps. The Dakota does not have cowl flaps, but for those airplanes that do, like the Cessna 182, cowl flaps should be open for ground operations, since this is the most difficult cooling situation for your engine. The point of your cowl flaps is to help regulate the temperature of your engine. By monitoring your cylinder head temperature, you can use your cowl flaps to help keep that temperature where you want it. You should open your cowl flaps for takeoff and climbs, and close them for cruise, descents and landings. Upon landing you should open them while taxiing in order to cool your engine. Some instructors recommend then closing them again upon tie down, to avoid birds or anything else getting into your engine compartment.

CARB HEAT - off

The carburetor has a heater associated with it to take care of any icing that might occur, which can block fuel flow to the engine. What causes icing in your carburetor? Vaporization of fuel and sudden expansion of air passing through the carburetor can result in sudden cooling of the fuel/air mixture by as much as 15°C. This cooling causes water to condense out of the air, and if the temperature reaches 0°C or below, ice will form inside the carburetor.

Be mindful of the possibility of carburetor icing in any condition where there is visible moisture or high humidity and the temperature is between -7°C and 21°C. The most serious potential problem arises during engine cooling upon landing, when you are close to the ground and would have to react particularly quickly to a serious reduction or loss of engine efficiency.

Since engine performance is slightly reduced by application of carb heat, it should be off for takeoff. Later in your checklist, you will check the operation of your carburetor heater by checking for an rpm drop when the heater is turned on, which is a manifestation of this reduction in engine performance.

PASSENGER BRIEF - complete

What if you had to perform a forced landing and were knocked unconscious in the process? Would your passengers know how to unbuckle their seatbelts and unlock the door? These items and anything else you think is vital to safety should be explained to your passengers before you takeoff. In the Dakota, the front door latches at the door handle and at the top of the door. If passengers were not aware of this, they may not escape the plane in a crash landing.

SEATS - locked

A number of accidents have occurred upon takeoff due to the pilot's seat not being locked on its tracks. A sudden sliding of the seat backward at the wrong moment on takeoff can totally disorient the pilot, resulting in a power on stall or some other disaster. Push your seat forward and back to make sure it is secure before you leave the ground. If you push back while applying your brakes, you conveniently test both your brake tension and that your seat is locked on its tracks.

SEATBELTS - secure

As in an automobile, in an airplane seat belts save lives, and their use is required by the FAA for everyone in the airplane, during taxiing on the ground, on takeoff, and upon landing.

CABIN DOOR - locked

The last thing you want to have happen is to have the cabin door open during takeoff. This would be extremely distracting at a critical time in your flight. What should you do if this actually happens? It's important to realize that this is more unnerving than necessarily dangerous. The wind keeps the door essentially closed, and when you reach altitude, you probably can level off, enter slow flight conditions, and then shut the door properly. If the wind still makes this difficult, you may want to consider returning for landing.

Photo by Uta Francke

Compliance with and
adherence to TCDS's, STC's
and AD's are required for your
aircraft to be airworthy. In addition,
all parts used to meet the compliance
requirements must be approved by
the FAA. If not, the airplane's
airworthiness certificate
becomes invalid.

ENGINE START

MIXTURE/PROP - full forward

What are you actually doing when you change your mixture control? In the simplest system, such as a Cessna 152, fuel flows by gravity from the high wings through first a shutoff valve, then a fuel strainer, and is then mixed with air in the carburetor. This fuel/air mixture then proceeds to the engine cylinders. Your mixture control operates at the level of the carburetor, simply adjusting how much air is getting mixed with the fuel. Mixture full forward means the maximum ratio of fuel to air at the carburetor, or full rich.

What are you actually doing when you change your prop control? There are two opposing forces that operate to maintain the blade angle of your propellers - a fixed force and a variable force. The fixed force often results by centrifugal force acting on counterweights, and it either increases or decreases the blade angle, depending on the design of your particular propeller. The variable force results from a variable amount of oil pressure on a piston operating in the propeller dome, and it counteracts the fixed force. A mechanical linkage connects the piston to the blades, and the linkage converts the linear motion of the piston into a rotary motion that changes the blade angle.

The propeller governor is connected to the engine drivetrain by a drive shaft. The governor's job is to sense the engine rpm and compare it to the rpm you have selected with the propeller control lever. It then directs oil pressure to or from the propeller dome, which causes the blade angle to change to maintain your selected rpm.

To understand the operation of your constant-speed propeller better, you need to know about the pilot valve, flyweights and the speeder spring, which are all part of the prop governor. It is the position of the pilot valve that determines whether oil is being directed to the propeller hub or back to the engine. The pilot valve position is controlled by flyweights that are mounted at the end of the drive shaft. The flyweights tilt outward as rpm increases and inward as it decreases. Associated with the flyweights is the speeder spring, which is connected to the cockpit propeller lever. When you push in the propeller lever to increase the rpm, you compress the speeder spring, which pushes down on the flyweights causing them to tilt inward. This inward tilt causes the pilot valve to move down, which permits oil to flow under pressure to the propeller dome. The oil pushes on the piston in the dome, which results in a decrease of the blade angle. This configuration results in less resistance on the blades, and the rpm of the propeller and the engine increases.

THROTTLE (IF THE ENGINE IS PARTICULARLY COLD, PUMP 1 TIME) - 1/4 inch open

What are you actually doing when you change your throttle control? The throttle, like the mixture control, is operating at the level of the carburetor, and simply determines how much of the fuel/air mixture is fed to the engine cylinders.

If you are flying a constant-speed prop airplane, you have a manifold pressure gauge that reads out the absolute pressure in the engine intake manifold. When you select a higher manifold pressure with the throttle, you are increasing the amount of fuel/air mixture that enters the cylinder for each intake stroke.

Some instructors teach their students not to open the throttle before cranking the engine but to push the throttle forward as the engine catches. This allows for a smoother start with an engine that does not rev when it's cold.

CARB HEAT - cold

Engine performance is slightly reduced by application of carb heat, and it should be off for startup and for takeoff.

PRIMER - 5 times if cold / 2 times if hot / lock

How does the manual single action piston pump, or primer, work? When you pull out the primer, you are sucking some fuel into the primer cylinder. When you push in the primer, you are forcing that fuel into the cylinders. This simple device is pretty foolproof, but you want to make sure that it is locked before takeoff, or else during takeoff fuel may flow into the primer cylinder rather than into the engine, resulting in an engine failure.

AUXILIARY FUEL PUMP - on

In a low wing aircraft it is impossible for the fuel to be taken to the engine by gravity, and your plane will have an engine driven fuel pump that pulls the fuel from your tank through your shutoff valve and fuel strainer into your carburetor.

If you have an auxiliary fuel pump, generally electrically driven, you can use it to prime your engine, in starting your engine, and as a backup in case of engine driven pump failure. At this point in your checklist, it is being used in conjunction with starting your engine.

An auxiliary fuel pump, mostly found in fuel injected aircraft, comes in extremely handy when you experience vapor lock in your lines. The presence of vapor lock in your lines prevents liquid fuel from traveling freely through your fuel line system. The time you are most likely to experience vapor lock is when you shut down your engine on a hot summer day. You are stationary and have no cooling airflow, the fuel lines under the hot cowling become hot, and vaporization of the fuel within occurs. You can crank your engine for a long time, wearing down your battery, without having successful engine start if you are using the normal start procedure.

With an auxiliary fuel pump you can easily flush the system and clear the lines of vapor. Whether or not you have an auxiliary fuel pump, you should understand the hot start procedure for your airplane.

PROPELLER AREA - clear

Given the severity and probable lethality of someone being struck by your propeller upon startup, give a loud shout "CLEAR!" before turning that starter key. Also, make sure that no one is behind the aircraft. They will be caught in the wash of the sudden movement of air backward as the engine engages.

BATTERY MASTER - on

When the battery half of the master switch is off, the battery is isolated from most of your electrically-driven instruments. This saves turning each instrument off individually after shutdown. Furthermore, your turn coordinator, for example, which has an electrically driven gyroscope, does not have its own on-off switch. Without the master switch off, such instruments will continue to drain power from the battery after shutdown. I said switching off the battery master switch turns off "most" of your electrical equipment. Usually some instruments, like a clock or courtesy light for entering and exiting the aircraft, are connected to a hot battery bus or essential bus. These are not turned off when the battery switch is off and continue to draw down on the battery. So be sure to turn these off when possible by their individual switches.

The battery is basically a device that converts chemical energy into electricity. A chemical reaction proceeds spontaneously, which generates energy that is converted into electricity. That electricity is used to start up your engine by cranking the starter motor. Once started, the battery serves as a backup of your alternator (see below) for powering all of your avionics, lights, and other electrical equipment.

Two terms you should understand are volts and amps. A volt is a measure of electrical potential, and is therefore the motivating force for moving electrical current through the conducting elements of your electrical system. An amp is a measure of the rate of that electrical flow, known as the current. An amp-hour is the rating given to a battery and indicates how long your battery will last without recharging it when drawing a particular current. If, for example, you have a 20 amp-hour battery, it will supply 5 amps of current for 4 hours.

ALTERNATOR SWITCH - on

Turning off the alternator half of the battery switch isolates your alternator from your electrical instruments and from the battery.

Since generally your current needs are more than 5 amps (see above), your battery will not last long without being recharged. This is one purpose of your alternator. As long as your engine is running and your alternator is working, your battery is being constantly recharged by the engine driven alternator. Basically, the alternator supplies electricity to the battery, and the input current reverses the battery's chemical reaction, which when running forward is used for engine startup. The alternator also generates sufficient current to handle the normal power requirements during your flight.

The alternator rotor requires magnetism to generate the lines of flux that are required to generate electricity. Before startup, there is no magnetic field available, and the alternator requires ~2 amps of current from the battery to activate the alternator's exciter field. Once the exciter field is activated, the engine operation causes the alternator rotor to turn, which generates electricity. The alternator then supplies its own 2 amps of excitation.

If your red light comes on or your ammeter is not reading in the positive, indicating that your alternator is inoperative, this does not mean that your alternator has necessarily failed. The first thing to do is check that your alternator half of your master switch hasn't been accidentally turned off. If the alternator circuit breaker has tripped, then try a reset. It may have been just a momentary glitch in your system. It might also be that the alternator is just "off line" (without necessarily tripping the circuit breaker), and what needs to be done is recycle the alternator, switching off and back on the alternator side of the master switch.

It is important to understand that should your alternator truly fail, your battery will work for a while as a backup, but the time left on the battery depends on the amp-hour rating of the battery and how much electrical demand in amps is being placed on it. This is why you shut down all unnecessary electrical equipment when you have an alternator failure. It is useful to generate a chart for each airplane you fly that indicates the amps needed for each electrical component of your airplane, and the groupings of instruments that are protected by a given circuit breaker (Figure 2). List them in the order that they appear on your panel at the top of your chart to make them easier to find. Under that, list them in order of their energy use. A quick glance at this chart shows the big energy users. Shut down all unnecessary equipment. In some instances, pulling the circuit breaker to turn off a bank of instruments is the easy way to go. In some cases, such as the turn coordinator, this is the only way to turn it off.

If your alternator fails, you should turn off the alternator half of the master switch and draw what electricity is needed from your battery. Why turn off the alternator switch when the alternator isn't working? The reason is that the exciter field of an inoperative alternator still demands current, and if not isolated from the battery, it will unnecessarily drain precious electricity from the battery.

A critical element in your electrical system is the voltage regulator. Its job is to be sure that your electrical system has a constant and

Pitch trim	Altntr field	Engine group	Fuel pump	Landing gear pump cont. / lights		Stall warning	A.C./air blower	Rotating beacon	Pitot heat	Turn & bank	Auto pilot	Start & Acc.	Loran
5	5	5	10	2		5	20	10	15	5	5	15	5

Instrument panel	Lights overhead	Nav lights	Anti Coll light	Landing light	Com 1	Com 2	ADF/MB	Audio panel	Nav 1	Nav 2	DME	Transponder	Radio lights
5	5	7 1/2	15	10	10	10	5	5	5	5	3	5	5

A.C./air blower	20
Pitot heat	15
Start & Acc.	15
Anti Coll light	15
Fuel pump	10
Rotating beacon	10
Landing light	10
Com 1	10
Com 2	10
Nav lights	7 1/2
Pitch trim	5
Altntr field	5
Engine group	5
Stall warning	5
Turn & bank	5
Auto pilot	5
Loran	5
Instrument panel	5
Lights overhead	5
ADF/MB	5
Audio panel	5
Nav 1	5
Nav 2	5
Transponder	5
Radio lights	5
DME	3
Landing gear pump cont. /lights	2

Fig. 2. Load shedding chart in the event of alternator failure for a Piper Dakota
  (Not to be used without verification of information from official sources)

appropriate source of voltage for all conditions of flight. In order for the alternator to recharge the battery, for example, the alternator output voltage must be regulated to be slightly higher than the battery voltage, in order to force feed the battery and reverse the battery's chemical reaction. A value of about 19% higher is generally used. Thus, a 12 volt battery will have an alternator output of 14.25 volts and a 24 volt battery will have an alternator output of 28.5 volts.

Given the above considerations, the polarity of your system is critical. If you are changing your battery, using an external battery boost, or carrying out a fast charge on your battery, make certain your polarity is correct! Otherwise you may cause permanent damage to various components of your electrical system.

BEACON LIGHTS - on

This is yet another way to alert walkers by that your airplane is about to become active.

STARTER - engage

What do you do if your engine doesn't start up as quickly as usual? You probably didn't prime enough and you should give your engine another one or two primes and try again. Whatever you do, do not keep cranking away for a prolonged period. Starter time limits are generally under one minute. Otherwise, your system will overheat, and you can burn out your starter - basically you melt the solder that holds the field and armature windings. There are three common reasons for lack of engine start:
  √   the fuel selector is in the off position
  √   the magnetos are off
  √   the mixture is in the full lean or cutoff position.
Check these before calling your local mechanic.

If you are forced to use a ground power unit to start your engine, be absolutely sure that your avionics are all off. They are easily damaged by high transient voltages that can occur in this situation. The other issues to be mindful of is that the voltage of the ground power unit must match that of your airplane's system, and that the polarity of the unit must match that of your system as well.

A note regarding starting your airplane with a ground power unit - *do not do so if your battery is completely dead.* Your engine will start, but your alternator won't work (remember that the alternator requires ~2 amps of current from the battery to activate the alternator's exciter field; see bottom of page 21). Thus, you will not be recharging your battery, and you will have no power to your electrical system. The same issue applies to starting the engine by manually hand propping the airplane when the battery is completely dead.

One thing to look for upon starting your engine is whether the paint on your cowling is starting to blister. What is that likely to mean? What would you do if that occurred? This is certain indication of an induction fire! You need to act quickly, and the solution is not to turn the ignition off, in which case you will likely watch your airplane burn to completion. The way to put out the fire is to continue cranking your starter motor to suck the flames back into the cylinders.

THROTTLE - 900 RPM

This is the best idling speed for the Dakota.

ENGINE INSTRUMENTS - check

Your engine instruments include a tachometer, manifold pressure gauge, oil pressure gauge, and oil temperature gauge. As the engine warms up, all instruments should be in the green.

OIL PRESSURE - in the green

Oil pressure is measured at the outlet of the engine-driven oil pump. Oil serves at least five critical purposes for your engine:

1. First and foremost it serves as a lubricant, reducing friction as metal moves against metal at high speeds during engine operation.

2. It also serves as a seal between the pistons and cylinder walls, providing maximum compression of the fuel/air mixture in the cylinder.

3. Since it is constantly being replaced in the cylinders with fresh oil, cooled by the oil cooler, it serves as a coolant. The oil cooler is a radiator that transfers the heat from the oil to the ram air from the outside.

4. It serves as a cleanser, gathering metal particles, dirt and water as it passes through the engine. Particulate matter is captured by the oil filter, which is important to change very regularly.

5. It prevents rust and corrosion by coating the metal surfaces and keeping moisture and contaminants away.

AUXILIARY FUEL PUMP - off

As discussed above, you want the auxiliary fuel pump on for startup, but for taxiing you want this pump off, and you should lean your mixture a bit to avoid spark plug fouling. Taxiing without your auxiliary pump on is a check that your engine driven pump is functioning properly on its own.

Given the severity and probable lethality of someone being struck by your propeller upon startup, give a loud shout "CLEAR!" before turning that starter key.

BEFORE TAXI

MIXTURE - lean

Lean your mixture as much as possible to avoid spark plug fouling.

TRANSPONDER 1200 - standby

The transponder is only useful to you and air traffic control when you are airborne.

RADIO MASTER - on

It is now safe to turn on your radio master. Your engine is running smoothly, and your battery is on and buffering any voltage spikes that might damage your avionics equipment.

AVIONICS - set / check

Set up the com and nav frequencies that are appropriate for the initial phase of your flight.

ATIS - copy

Copy the automatic terminal information service (ATIS) information. See Chapter 3 for a recommended Progress of Flight Chart on which you can write this information.

ALTIMETER - set

If your airport of departure does not have an ATIS that reports your atmospheric pressure setting, then set your altimeter based on the known altitude of the airport.

DIRECTIONAL GYRO - set

Before taxiing, you set your directional gyro to the heading indicated on your magnetic compass. This is the time to be sure your magnetic compass is working properly. Verify the accuracy of your magnetic compass by checking its magnetic indication on known headings. This is easily done, for example on a runway or taxiway. Another thing to be sure of is that you have sufficient compass fluid.

Once, on a planned IFR departure from St. Louis to Denver, my compass fluid was low enough that the compass was not moving completely freely. If I were in a hurry, I could have easily missed this. I immediately shut down and contacted the local mechanic. Refilling the magnetic compass and making certain all the seals were tight was a much larger task than I had anticipated. It was interesting to watch the operation, and I gained respect for the internal workings of the magnetic compass. It took three hours before I was off on my trip, but flying IFR circumnavigating thunderstorms across Kansas with a compass that wasn't working perfectly would have been an exhausting and dangerous experience.

Since your vacuum pump can fail, resulting in loss of your directional gyro, all pilots should know how to use the magnetic compass and to time standard rate turns in order to change headings. This simple procedure is often taught only during IFR training. Remember that a standard rate turn is 360° in 2 minutes. This corresponds to 3° per second. Thus, if you are flying a heading of 090° and you want to make a left turn to 060°, or 30° to the left, put your airplane into a standard rate turn and count to 10 (pronouncing 1001, 1002, 1003, ... is a good estimate of counting off seconds). With a little practice, you will be amazed how accurate this can be. But don't forget that your compass is only accurate in straight and level, unaccelerated flight.

FLIGHT INSTRUMENTS - check

Set and check the remainder of your flight instruments - airspeed indicator, attitude indicator, altimeter, turn coordinator, and vertical speed indicator.

FUEL SELECTOR - fullest tank

Fuel starvation is the cause of so many unnecessary accidents. You will notice that this check appears multiple times on my checklist.

Photo by James Spudich

Since your vacuum pump can fail, resulting in loss of your directional gyro, all pilots should know how to use the magnetic compass and to time standard rate turns in order to change headings.

TAXI

<u>BRAKES</u> - check

On a flight from Montana to California in a Cessna 182, I landed for fuel in Winnemucca, Nevada. It was clear upon landing that my right brake was completely nonfunctional. After a left 270 on the runway using my left brake, I taxied off the runway to transient parking and found the local mechanic. He quickly discovered that I had been losing brake fluid as a result of a small hole in the brake fluid line that runs under the wheel strut. This experience emphasized, once again, how important it is to do an extremely thorough external preflight check. Surely there must have been some drops of brake fluid under this wheel strut when I left the airport at Great Falls.

Why is the brake fluid, better known as hydraulic fluid, so critical for brake function? Hydraulics is one of the wonders of physics. The hydraulic fluid in your closed brake system is an incompressible fluid. When you apply a force to that fluid, by pushing on your toe brakes, that pressure is felt everywhere in your brake system instantaneously. No fluid has to actually flow to your brake pads. It is simply the pressure that is transmitted. Thus, there is minimal friction involved and therefore very little energy is lost as heat. So the brake system is very simple. You press forward on the toe pads. This pushes down on a moving piston in your master cylinder, which puts pressure on the hydraulic fluid within. This pressure is transmitted through the hydraulic tubing to your brake housing, which again has a piston and pads. The piston responds to the increased pressure by pushing against linings that cause friction, which stops your wheel motion.

MAGNETIC COMPASS, ATTITUDE INDICATOR, DIRECTIONAL GYRO, TURN COORDINATOR, VERTICAL SPEED INDICATOR - check

As you taxi and make a turn, check that these five instruments are behaving properly. The magnetic compass and directional gyro should turn to reflect your new heading. The turn coordinator should indicate your turn, but your attitude indicator should not -- the attitude indicator should reflect the fact that your wings are level and you are neither ascending or descending. The vertical speed indicator should be reading zero.

TAKEOFF BRIEFING - complete

Inform your passengers that you are about to takeoff, make sure their seat belts are fastened, and generally check on their well being.

The hydraulic fluid in your closed brake system is an incompressible fluid. When you apply a force to that fluid, by pushing on your toe brakes, that pressure is felt everywhere in your brake system instantaneously. No fluid has to actually flow to your brake pads. It is simply the pressure that is transmitted.

BEFORE TAKEOFF

FLIGHT CONTROLS - correct

I check full range of motion and turn the yoke full left. Looking out the left window I say "up" and looking out the right window I say "down" [the position of the ailerons if they are *correctly connected* to the yoke]. I repeat this with full right yoke, looking first out of the right window - "up" - and then the left window - "down." I then check the elevator and rudder pedals.

MIXTURE - rich

You are about to do your high power runup. So your mixture should be full rich (unless you are at a high altitude airport, in which case you need to lean to best power).

THROTTLE - 2000 RPM

The starred items below need to be checked at high engine power.

*MAGNETOS (175 RPM MAXIMUM DROP, 50 RPM MAXIMUM DIFFERENCE BETWEEN MAGNETOS) - check

An airplane engine in many ways is like a car engine. But what happens in your car if your alternator/battery system goes dead while traveling? Your engine immediately stops because the spark plugs are no longer getting needed energy to ignite the fuel/air mixture. This scenario is not tolerable in flight. If your alternator/battery system dies in your airplane, you will lose all electrical power to your instruments, but your engine will continue to run. How is this achieved? This is what your magnetos are for. They are solely responsible for igniting the fuel/air mixture in the engine's cylinders.

The FAA requires that every certified airplane has two magnetos per engine.

The magnetos create their own voltage by the relative movement of a conductor and a magnetic field. This relative movement is driven by the engine operation. Each cylinder of your engine has two spark plugs and two wiring harnesses that connect the spark plugs to the magnetos. The magnetos create sufficient voltage to jump the spark plug gap, which guarantees proper fuel/air mixture combustion. Thus, as long as your engine is running, it is driving your magnetos, which keep the engine running. Furthermore, two magnetos gives you back up, since the airplane will continue to operate on only one. Note, however, that using one set up spark plugs is not as efficient as using both. Thus, if you turn one magneto off, you will notice some drop in rpm as a result of incomplete combustion. This is of course familiar to you, because you check for this rpm drop in your run-up before takeoff.

A primary wire or P-lead connects each magneto to ground by way of the magneto switch. The P-lead simply provides a path of least resistance, such that a magneto is inoperative when the switch is turned off. Thus , when you select one magneto, you are grounding that magneto and therefore turning it off. It is critical to realize that if your P-lead breaks or comes detached from its ground point on the fuselage, that magneto will be hot even when the ignition switch is turned completely off. This is an incredibly dangerous situation, because your propeller is directly connected to your engine and any manipulation of your propeller that turns over the engine can activate the magneto to fire the spark plugs and your engine will come to life. This loss of grounding due to a P-lead break is easily caught, because you'll have no rpm drop when you select that magneto in your run-up test.

If you don't understand the system, you may not pay attention to this lack of rpm drop, which places you and others in serious danger with the risk of serious injury or even death resulting from a sudden coming to life of your engine in what you thought was a completely docile, shut down airplane. In my 30 years of flying, I have only experienced this once. Understanding the system, I simply checked under the hood, noticed a disconnected P-lead, walked over to tell the mechanic who normally serviced my airplane, and after a quick fix was on my way. The entire delay was no more than 20 minutes.

What does it mean if your engine runs rough when you select a particular magneto? This is a sure sign of spark plug fouling, which means carbon has deposited on the spark plug, probably as a result of excessively rich mixture. Spending too much time on the ground with an idling engine with your mixture rich will surely foul your spark plugs. You can burn off much of the carbon on the spark plug by increasing your power setting and use the leanest mixture setting possible without killing your engine. Wait for 10 or 15 seconds, and then return to normal power settings and recheck your mag.

*PROP (CHECK FOR RPM DROP, OIL PRESSURE GAUGE TWITCH, MANIFOLD PRESSURE INCREASE) - cycle 3x

By cycling the props, you are circulating the engine warmed oil through the propeller system. Cold oil is sluggish, and changes in the prop blade angle, driven by oil pressure acting on the propeller and controlled by the prop governor, need to occur quickly and smoothly under your control.

Pulling back on your prop control increases the pitch angle of the propeller, and therefore reduces the speed at which it and the engine is turning. Thus, the rpm drops. Anytime you change the pitch of the propeller, oil is being inserted into or released from the prop hub. Thus you should see a twitch on your oil pressure gauge, unless your gauge is not sensitive enough. The manifold pressure should increase as you pull back on the prop control, because the velocity of air going in the venturi decreases as a result of the slower propeller. Therefore, the pressure measured past the venturi is higher. Note that many instructors teach cycling the props only once or at most twice. They argue that three times is not necessary and it's hard on the propeller system.

An important check that is often overlooked is to check proper operation of the governor. To do this, bring the power to 2200 rpm with the throttle. Then reduce the rpm to 1800 using the prop control. Now advance the MP and make sure the governor is keeping the rpm set at 1800.

*CARB HEAT (~100 RPM DROP) - check, cold

Application of carb heat causes a loss of efficiency of your engine operation, which causes an rpm drop. Thus, this drop indicates that your carb heat is working.

*ENGINE GAUGES - check

At this point your engine and its oil are fully warmed and all of your engine instruments should be in the green.

*AMMETER, ALTERNATOR - check

Most airplanes that you fly have a zero center type of ammeter, which is in the battery charging circuit, and therefore reflects the charge state of the battery. A positive indication means the alternator is working and is supplying electricity to the battery. A negative reading means that the alternator is not operating and the battery is being discharged, supplying electricity to your system.

Another type of alternator indicator is the zero left loadmeter type. This instrument simply indicates the amount of load on the alternator and does not indicate the charge state of the battery. The following questions assume a zero center type ammeter.

What does it mean if:
1. your ammeter indicates a negative (left) reading when the

startup motor is engaged? This is normal - you are drawing current from the battery for engine startup.

2. your ammeter indicates a negative (left) reading anytime after engine start? This is a problem - your alternator is not functioning.

3. your ammeter indicates a positive (right) reading right after startup? This is normal - your alternator is recharging your battery.

4. your ammeter indicates a positive (right) full scale reading that lasts for more than a minute after startup? This is a problem. Your starter motor is still engaged. Shut down and have a mechanic check this out.

5. your ammeter indicates a positive (right) reading well into your cruise flight? This is a problem - it probably indicates voltage regulator problems, causing the alternator to overcharge the battery. This can have serious consequences. A primary concern is that the overvoltage may damage various components of your electrical system. The battery can also overheat and even explode. If a reset doesn't work, turn off the alternator, reduce your electrical needs as much as possible, and land as soon as possible.

*VACUUM (4-6" MERCURY)/ALTERNATE STATIC PORT - check both

Why does your vacuum pump reading go up when you increase your power? The answer is that the pump is engine driven, and you therefore pull more vacuum at higher engine power. Which instruments will become non-operational if you lose your vacuum pump? The answer is your attitude indicator and your directional gyro. But do you know why? The answer is that these two instruments operate by gyroscopes spinning within, which transmit to you an indication of attitude and direction.

These gyroscopes, unlike the electrically driven gyroscope in your turn coordinator, are driven by cabin air that is pulled through the gyros and into the pump, assuming you have a conventional vacuum type system. If the pump is of the wet type, it uses engine oil for both lubrication and cooling. As air is pulled into the pump, an oil separator returns most of the oil to the engine and exhausts the air out of the system. You may have a dry pump, which is simpler, lighter, and self lubricating.

Note that vacuum pumps have a limited lifetime, and 500 hours of use is getting on. Make sure your vacuum pump reads 4-6 inches mercury during your runup. Upon reducing the throttle, check when the vacuum falls below 4 inches. It should stay between 4-6 inches all the way down to 1000 rpm. Also unusual behavior of your attitude indicator (it should not show a significant change in attitude while taxiing on the ground) or excessive precession of your directional gyro are signs of possible imminent vacuum pump failure.

THROTTLE - 900 RPM

Your high power check is finished. Throttle back to idle.

FUEL SELECTOR, AUXILIARY PUMP - on fullest tank, on

Fuel starvation is the cause of so many unnecessary accidents. This check appears multiple times on my checklist. Your auxiliary fuel pump should be on for takeoff as a backup for your engine driven fuel pump, should the latter fail in this critical phase of flight.

In order to check proper functioning of both tanks, some instructors suggest taxiing on one tank until reaching the run-up area, and then switching to the other tank to do the actual run-up. This gives you a good indication that both tanks work, that your fuel selector valve is operational, and that you have no contamination in your fuel.

TRIM - just aft of neutral

Neutral trim in many airplanes is appropriate for a proper, virtually unassisted takeoff when you reach the appropriate speed. For Pipers, slightly aft of neutral should generally be used.

TRANSPONDER - on Altitude, squawk 1200

ATC requires an altitude encoding transponder in many situations and always benefits from information about your position as soon as you takeoff.

ANNUNCIATOR PANEL - set

It is time to tune in the tower or the otherwise appropriate communication frequency for takeoff.

FLIGHT INSTRUMENTS - set, check

Do a final reset and check of all of your flight instruments.

PRIMER - in, locked

You want to make sure that the primer is in and locked before takeoff, or else during takeoff fuel may flow into the primer cylinder rather than into the engine, resulting in an engine failure.

LIGHTS - as required

You should always use position lights and anticollision lights.

DOORS, WINDOWS, BELTS - secure

This is a final check of these important items before takeoff.

AUTOPILOT - off

You want to be in complete control of your airplane upon takeoff.

TIME OFF - note

It's essential to note your time of takeoff for proper fuel consumption calculations and for determining the time to change tanks.

It is critical to realize that if your P-lead breaks or comes detached from its ground point on the fuselage, that magneto will be hot even when the ignition switch is turned completely off. This is an incredibly dangerous situation.

NORMAL TAKEOFF

FLAPS - up

Flaps should be up since you don't want drag when you take off, which is a primary function of flaps used for landing. But on most Cessnas and Pipers, flap extension also extends the wing surface somewhat and therefore provides some lift. You use this when you carry out a short field takeoff, which generally calls for 10 - 25° of flaps, where you obtain the best ratio of lift to drag.

ROTATE - 65 KIAS

Interestingly, this is your first test of proper operation of your pitot-static system. If you rely on your airspeed indications for takeoff, climb, cruise, descent and landing, someday you may find yourself in big trouble. You must learn to fly by the sound of your engine and all the visual clues available to you in VFR flight. Or do you believe that nothing can ever go wrong with your pitot-static system?

Your pitot-static system consists of your altimeter, your vertical speed indicator and your airspeed indicator. The altimeter is a simple instrument which has an evacuated diaphragm that expands as you climb due to a decrease in atmospheric pressure. The diaphragm is linked to a rocking shaft, which causes the needles on the face of your instrument to turn. Very little goes wrong with this instrument, but it's critical to be clear what it is actually displaying. The altimeter displays indicated altitude. This value must be corrected for installation error to give you your calibrated altitude - generally a small correction. This must then be corrected for nonstandard atmospheric conditions to give you your true altitude, which is your actual height above mean sea level. This correction is made by obtaining the atmospheric pressure reading for your location and dialing that value into the Kollsman window on your altimeter.

The vertical speed indicator measures the rate of change of the ambient static pressure, which is converted to feet per minute of climb or descent on the face of the instrument. This instrument also has an internal diaphragm, but in this case as the altitude changes, the diaphragm responds to the free-flowing static pressure. Note that the vertical speed indicator gives you a good reference for level flight, which is a backup for your attitude indicator (which is nonfunctional if your vacuum pump ceases to function).

Your airspeed indicator basically measures the difference between the ambient air pressure, or the static pressure, and the air pressure that results from the airplane moving through the air, or the ram air pressure. The ram air pressure is measured by the pitot tube, which is generally fixed to the underside of the left wing.

If you neglect to check the pitot tube carefully on your external preflight, you may miss that it has a bug in the tube or some trapped water. Anything blocking the pitot tube will essentially transform your airspeed indicator into an altimeter. Needless to say, your airspeed readings are going to be very different from what you expect. The design of the instrument is such that a blocked pitot tube would cause an apparent increase in airspeed as you climb, and an apparent decrease as you descend.

If the airspeed indicator is behaving in this fashion, you should cover the instrument until you have a chance to land and clear the pitot tube.

You can also have faulty airspeed indications if your static port is blocked. Check whether opening your alternate static port solves the problem. What do you mean that you don't know where this port is? But if that's true, you are not alone. This cockpit item is often ignored by pilots. When was the last time you checked the alternate static system in your preflight?

If you need to switch to your alternate static system, you should remember that this source is usually vented to the pressure inside the cockpit. The pressure inside the cockpit is usually lower than the pressure provided by the normal static air source, due to the Venturi effect of the flow of air over the cockpit. Thus, when using the alternate static source, the altimeter will indicate higher than the actual altitude, the airspeed indicator will indicate greater than the actual airspeed, and the vertical speed indicator will indicate a climb when you are in level flight.

CLIMB OUT - 80 KIAS

The oil temperature gauge is a critical monitor of your engine performance. It should be in the green before takeoff. If during climb out an excessively high oil temperature develops, then you should proceed by step climbing. That is, reduce your power and level off to increase your airspeed, and therefore your cooling air flow, which will allow your temperature to return to the normal range. Climb again, and repeat the procedure.

AT 500 FEET AGL, SET MANIFOLD PRESSURE, PROP RPM - 25, 2400

The normal climb configuration for the Dakota is 25 inches manifold pressure and 2400 rpm. Wait until you are 500 feet above ground level (AGL) because you want some height in the event of engine failure. You should always be aware that the most common time for an unexpected engine failure is when you are making changes to your power settings.

AT 1000 FEET AGL (FUEL PUMP, LANDING LIGHT) - both off

Now that your airplane has adjusted to the new power settings, turn off your auxilliary fuel pump, which should not be needed if your engine driven pump is working properly. But again, it's important to be aware that changes in the fuel pump system also may result in engine failure. If that happened at this point, simply turning the auxilliary fuel pump back on is likely to solve the problem. But returning to the airport to get your engine driven fuel pump checked out would be in order.

Landing lights are generally useless after leaving the runway at night and can even be distracting if you have any light fog or smog. But if there is a lot of traffic in your area, you may choose to leave your lights on until getting away from the busy airspace you find yourself in - even in daytime. This helps to be seen by other aircraft.

If you rely on your airspeed indications for takeoff, climb, cruise, descent and landing, someday you may find yourself in big trouble. You must learn to fly by the sound of your engine and all the visual clues available to you in VFR flight.

CRUISE

CRUISE POWER - 24, 2400

24 inches MP and 2400 rpm props are normal cruise power settings for the Dakota at low altitudes. These values, however, are clearly altitude dependent. Check the POH.

What should you do if you experience a partial loss of power during flight? Prepare for a precautionary landing. If time permits, your knowledge of systems should have you:
1. checking and adjusting the mixture control
2. checking your fuel levels and switching tanks
3. checking and applying carb heat
4. checking that the manual fuel primer is full in and locked
5. checking the function of your magnetos by cycling among the three positions - both, left and right

LANDING LIGHTS - off

In the event that you left your lights on in order to be seen better in busy airspace, once you are clear of that airspace, the lights should go off. You want to save them for when you may need them for descent into busy airspace again or for landing.

MIXTURE - lean

If your aircraft has a fixed pitch propeller, then you will commonly use the engine roughness technique for leaning your mixture. That is, you lean your mixture until the engine runs a bit rough, and then you increase the richness of your mixture by about two turns.

But if your airplane has an exhaust gas temperature measuring gauge (EGT), it should be used for proper mixture control. The amount of heat produced by your fuel combustion depends sensitively on the fuel/air ratio. At peak EGT, the maximum number of fuel and oxygen molecules react. Generally, manufacturers recommend operating at best power, which is achieved by enriching the mixture so that EGT is about 100°F cooler than peak EGT.

GAUGES - check

An indication of zero oil pressure and oil temperature rising during flight mandates immediate landing. The most common problem for such a reading is insufficient oil, and your engine will not operate for long without proper oil lubrication. If oil pressure is zero but oil temperature is normal, then chances are your oil pressure gauge is not functioning normally. In this situation, land as soon as possible and have a mechanic check it out.

What should you do if you notice unusually high CHT readings while in flight? The usual problem is that your mixture is too lean. This is easily corrected by simply enriching your mixture.

Is your heater working properly? Assuming you have an exhaust manifold heater, you are drawing heat into the cabin directly from a shroud that is placed around the engine exhaust stack and picking up the heat from the engine's exhaust system. What is the worst possible danger with this system? Carbon monoxide, the silent killer, could leak into your heating system if there is a leak between the manifold and the exhaust pipe and thus into the cabin. Having a relatively new carbon monoxide detector (they lose their effectiveness with time) in the airplane in plain site is a must.

During cruise flight you notice a smell of burned oil and unusually high oil and cylinder head temperatures for the normal settings that you use. What should you do? This is a sign of a potentially serious engine problem and calls for reducing power, landing as soon as possible, and having your engine checked out by a mechanic. The same advice applies to an unexpected unusual vibration, which may be a result of engine problems. While icing or a loose control surface could also cause the plane to vibrate, you are not likely to be able to troubleshoot the problem in the air. Land as soon as possible.

Suppose during cruise you discover a decrease in both EGT and CHT. What might this imply? The most obvious problem would be some form of fuel system blockage, for example due to icing.

An increase in both EGT and CHT, on the other hand, would indicate preignition. Preignition occurs when the fuel/air mixture is ignited prior to spark plug discharge. It can be caused by a hot spot in the cylinder, which is often the result of carbon buildup. If this occurs, you should reduce CHT immediately by enriching the mixture, opening cowl flaps if you have them, and reducing the power. Land as soon as possible, and have a mechanic take a look.

What if you notice an increase in CHT and a decrease in EGT? This would indicate an explosive detonation of the fuel/air mixture in the engine cylinders. This usually occurs at high power settings, and is often the consequence of improper leaning. This situation is not an efficient use of fuel, so the cylinder head temperature goes up while the exhaust gas temperature goes down. Again, it is important to reduce CHT immediately, land as soon as possible, and have a mechanic take a look.

Any indication of zero oil pressure during flight mandates immediate landing. The most common problem for such a reading is insufficient oil, and your engine will not operate for long without proper oil lubrication.

CRUISE CLIMB

POWER (MANIFOLD PRESSURE/ RPM) - 25/ 2400

MP 25 inches and 2400 rpm props are standard climb settings for the Dakota at low altitudes. These values, however, are clearly altitude dependent. Check the POH.

MIXTURE - rich/ as required

In the Dakota, if you are below 5000 feet MSL, the mixture should be full rich for a climb to ensure adequate fuel for the higher power settings and to facilitate some cooling of the engine. At higher altitudes, good climb power still allowing cooling will be achieved by leaning the mixture as required.

If your airplane has an exhaust gas temperature measuring gauge (EGT), it should be used for proper mixture control. The amount of heat produced by your fuel combustion depends sensitively on the fuel/air ratio. At peak EGT, the maximum number of fuel and oxygen molecules react.

DESCENT

FUEL SELECTOR - fullest tank

Descending usually means preparation for landing. You certainly want to land on the fullest tank, and you do not want to be changing tanks in the pattern. So now is the time to do it.

MIXTURE - increase richness as required

Gradually increasing the richness of the mixture as you descend helps to keep the engine temperature change gradual.

DESCENT POWER - set

Reduce power in increments. A good way to do this is to check the EGT and make sure the temperature does not decrease too fast. Otherwise, reduce the manifold pressure by 2 inches every two minutes. The point is to avoid long descents with the engine at idle, since the engine will cool too rapidly resulting in thermal shock. Keep the engine instruments in the green.

AVIONICS - set

Set your coms and navs appropriately to be ready for landing, starting with the ATIS frequency.

ATIS - copy

Copy the ATIS well ahead of landing and understand which runway you are landing on and the conditions of the airport. Of particular interest are the winds - what will your cross component wind velocity be on landing?

ALTIMETER - set

You need to be sure that your altimeter is reading out as close to true altitude as possible. This is the time to adjust your altimeter according to the atmospheric pressure reported in the ATIS.

LIGHTS - on

If it is night time or if you are flying into particularly busy airspace, then this is a good time to turn on your landing lights. Any other lights needed for your approach should be turned on at this time.

ENGINE INSTRUMENTS - check

Landing is the worst time to be surprised by some problem. Check now that all instruments are in the green.

FLIGHT INSTRUMENTS - check

Again, landing is the worst time to be surprised by some problem. Check now that all instruments are behaving normally and make any necessary adjustments, such as correcting a precessed directional gyro.

APPROACH BRIEFING - complete

All seat belts should be fastened and any information that you deem useful should be passed on to your passengers - for example, ATC instructions to hold or to enter an unusual pattern. Passengers get less nervous if they know what is going on.

APPROACH

LANDING LIGHT - on

If it is night time or if you are flying into particularly busy airspace, then double check that your landing lights are on.

FUEL (SELECTOR, AUXILIARY PUMP) - fullest tank, on

You certainly want to land on the fullest tank. Check again that you are on the fullest tank. You do not want to be changing tanks in the pattern.

Photo by James Spudich

Copy the ATIS well ahead of landing and understand which runway you are landing on and the conditions of the airport. Of particular interest are the winds - what will your cross component wind velocity be on landing?

BEFORE LANDING (ON DOWNWIND)

CARB HEAT - off / or as required

Unlike the Cessnas, the Piper Dakota does not recommend carb heat on for landing unless it is needed. Landing in cold, moist weather may call for turning it on.

FUEL (SELECTOR, AUXILIARY PUMP) - fullest tank, on

This is the final check that your fuel supply system is optimally configured for landing.

UNDERCARRIAGE - down, locked, green light

The gear is fixed in the Dakota, but I go through this check anyway so I am fully in the habit when I fly retractible gear airplanes.

MIXTURE - rich

Mixture rich is the normal situation for landing. If you are at a high altitude runway, you need to lean the mixture appropriately so that you land with best power.

PROPS/ PRIMER - full forward, locked

Props should be full forward mainly because you want that configuration should you need to carry out a go-around procedure. This way you are ready for that possibility. In noise sensitive areas, wait until your manifold pressure is at or below 15 inches before applying full forward props. This reduces noise pollution.

SEAT BELTS - on

This is not only sensible for safety, but required by FAA regulations.

Photo by Uta Francke

NORMAL LANDING

DOWNWIND (MANIFOLD PRESSURE, FLAPS) - 20, 0°

These are the appropriate settings in the Dakota for setting up your conditions for landing at the right speed, attitude and descent rate.

ABEAM THE RUNWAY NUMBERS (MANIFOLD PRESSURE, FLAPS) - 15, 10°

These are the appropriate settings in the Dakota for setting up your conditions for landing at the right speed, attitude and descent rate.

BASE (FLAPS AS REQUIRED) - 80 KIAS

Depending on weather conditions, adjust your flaps for appropriate conditions for landing at the right speed, attitude and descent rate.

FINAL APPROACH (FLAPS 40°) - 72 KIAS

These are the usual appropriate settings in the Dakota for setting up your conditions for landing at the right speed, attitude and descent rate. In very high winds, you may choose not to use full flaps. Also, remember to occasionally practice landing without any flaps, since you want to be able to do this with ease should you lose your flap controls.

Once, on a small commercial airliner flying into one of my favorite islands, I was allowed to sit in the copilot seat. I was returning home after a scientific meeting with several of my scientific colleagues, who were in the back seats. On final approach, the pilot tried to lower all the flaps. There was a very loud crackling noise, as the flap rod broke. As the pilot initiated a go-around, my colleagues immediately behind me tapped me on my shoulder to inquire what happened. I signaled to them that everything was OK and that they shouldn't be alarmed. I then asked the pilot whether in fact the flap rod broke. He said, "Yes, what do you think we should do?!" Somewhat startled by this question, I replied that I would fly to the nearby airport that I was familiar with, which has a much longer runway. The runway we were flying into was very short and had high tension wires near the end of the runway, essentially requiring a short field landing where flaps are very useful. The pilot indicated that he would give this runway one more try, and proceeded to make a perfect landing using up less than two thirds of the runway. I then realized that his question was in jest, and he was in complete control the entire time, having practiced no flap landings at this airport in this airplane many times before. With my personal level of skill at that time, I would have certainly diverted to the longer runway.

SHORT FINAL (GEAR DOWN, LOCKED & GREEN LIGHT, PROPS FULL FORWARD) - 72 KIAS

Again, so that I'm in the right habit when I fly retractable gear airplanes, on short final I always say aloud while I do the checks "Gear down, locked and green, props full forward" or "Gear down, locked and not green because this is a fixed gear airplane, props full forward."

LANDING - 72 KIAS

This is the appropriate landing speed for the Dakota , under normal conditions. With gusty winds, remember to add a few knots. The rule is to add one-half the difference between the wind speed and the gust speed. Thus, if the winds were 15 knots gusting to 25 knots, you would add 5 knots to your landing speed.

GO-AROUND

THROTTLE - full forward

You want full throttle, of course, and this is the first action to take for the go-around.

FLAPS - to 25°

Remember that flaps provide both drag and lift in many airplanes. Thus, if you fully retract your flaps, your loss of lift could easily have you quickly pointing toward the ground. Retracting your flaps to 25° in the Dakota reduces much of your drag without much loss of lift.

UNDERCARRIAGE - up

Gear down is a very large source of drag, and you should raise the gear at this point if you are in a retractible gear airplane. The Dakota has fixed gear, but I keep this on all my checklists just so I stay in the habit of checking the gear. That way, I am less likely to forget this when I do fly retractible gear airplanes.

PITCH - 75 KIAS, then 85 KIAS

75 KIAS is near the best angle of climb (Vx) for the Dakota, and 85 KIAS is the best rate (Vy).

FLAPS AT POSITIVE VSI AND REACHING Vy - retract

Remember that flaps provide both drag and lift in many airplanes. It is safe to remove all flaps once you have positive vertical speed indication and have reached Vy.

AFTER LANDING

FLAPS - up

Now that you are on the ground, it makes good sense to ready the airplane for the next takeoff. This is good pilot procedure.

TRIMS - set for takeoff

Now that you are on the ground, it makes good sense to ready the airplane for the next takeoff.

MIXTURE - lean

This will help prevent spark plug fouling.

CARB HEAT - off

Now that you are on the ground, it makes good sense to ready the airplane for the next takeoff, and carb heat is not needed at this time.

TRANSPONDER - standby

Why have ATC picking up your transponder while taxiing? They have enough to deal with already.

LIGHTS - as required

The high intensity strobe lights should be turned off while taxiing after landing. They can be blinding to other pilots operating near you, and can give airplanes in flight or on approach the illusion that you are on the runway, having just landed or getting ready to take off.

FUEL PUMP - off

Turn off the auxiliary fuel pump. You are now on the ground and are no longer worried about possible loss of your engine driven fuel pump or some other sudden reduction in fuel supply.

Remember to occasionally practice landing without any flaps, since you want to be able to do this with ease should you lose your flap controls.

SHUTDOWN

AVIONICS MASTER SWITCH, ALL ELECTRICAL - off (except for beacon)

Now that you are on the ground, it makes good sense to ready the airplane for the next takeoff. And you don't want your avionics system to experience damaging voltage fluctuations that can occur. I leave the beacon light on as long as the propeller is turning to alert anyone on foot near my plane.

THROTTLE - 900 rpm

The appropriate rpm for shutdown for the Dakota.

MIXTURE - idle cut-off

Mixture to idle cut-off starves the engine of fuel, and is the proper shutdown procedure in general. Leaving unnecessary fuel in the engine is undesirable - it's flammable!

BEACON AT KEY REMOVAL - off

I leave the beacon light on as long as the propeller is turning to alert anyone on foot near my airplane. I leave it on until I remove the key from the ignition switch.

MAGNETOS - off

Remember, magnetos on means an engine can start up by someone gently moving the prop by hand.

MASTER SWITCH - off

I have found a drained battery on more than one occasion, due to pilots who flew rental airplanes before me neglecting to turn off the master switch.

CONTROL LOCK - secure

I have found on many occasions that the pilot before me failed to secure the control lock. In a gusty wind condition, this mistake can result in serious damage to the elevator and aileron systems.

LOG - time

Take the time to fill out your log book now. You may not remember everything correctly if you wait to get home or wherever your final destination is.

COVERS (WINDOWS, NOSE VENTS, PITOT TUBE) - install

These are other items that I quite often find left undone by the previous pilot of a rental airplane.

POSTFLIGHT INSPECTION - clean up

Be courteous to others. Remove debris from the airplane and organize those items that are to remain within.

DOORS - lock

Another item that I quite often find left undone by the previous pilot of a rental airplane. Airplane avionics theft from airplanes is not uncommon.

TIE DOWNS - secure

It may not be gusty when you parked the airplane, but weather conditions can change very quickly.

Photo by Uta Francke

**Mixture to idle cut-off
starves the engine of fuel, and is the
proper shutdown procedure in general.
Leaving unnecessary fuel in the engine
is undesirable - it's flammable!**

SHORT FIELD TAKEOFF

FLAPS SECOND NOTCH - 25°

Give yourself that little extra lift that we discussed earlier.

MAXIMUM USABLE RUNWAY/ BRAKES - hold

Give yourself that little extra runway.

THROTTLE - full forward

Develop maximum power before releasing your brakes and using up any runway.

BRAKES - release

Now you are ready for your takeoff roll.

ELEVATOR CONTROL - keep in tail-low attitude

Reduce some of your drag by taking weight off your main gear.

ROTATE - 50-60 KIAS

Reduce some of your drag by getting the plane off the ground as soon as possible.

CLIMB OUT - 73 KIAS

This is the best angle of climb in the Dakota.

AFTER CLEARING 50-FOOT OBSTACLE - 85 KIAS

This is the best rate of climb in the Dakota.

Photo by James Spudich

Flying, like mountain climbing, is an exhilarating experience - but in the plane you can continue to climb above the summit

SHORT FIELD LANDING

DOWNWIND (MANIFOLD PRESSURE, FLAPS) - 20, 0°

These are the same settings as for a normal landing in the Dakota and are appropriate conditions for landing at the right speed, attitude and descent rate.

ABEAM THE RUNWAY NUMBERS (MANIFOLD PRESSURE, FLAPS) - 15, 10°

These are the same settings as for a normal landing in the Dakota and are appropriate conditions for landing at the right speed, attitude and descent rate.

BASE (FLAPS AS REQUIRED) - 80 KIAS

These are the same settings as for a normal landing in the Dakota. Depending on weather conditions, adjust your flaps for appropriate conditions for landing at the right speed, attitude and descent rate.

FINAL APPROACH (FULL FLAPS, GEAR DOWN, LOCKED & GREEN LIGHT, PROPS FULL FORWARD) - 65 KIAS

This is a slower approach speed than for a normal landing in the Dakota. This will enable you in part to land with less landing roll than usual.

SHALLOW APPROACH UNLESS OBSTACLES - 65 KIAS

Use a shallow final approach, unless you have obstacles in your path.

POWER - some

More than normal power is held while trimmed for 65 KIAS, right down to the runway. This is the major reason that you will land with less landing roll than usual. When you reach the runway and pull your throttle back to full stop, the sudden loss of power puts you in essentially stall condition as soon as you touch the ground.

LANDING - 50-65 KIAS

Landing at this speed under the conditions described above means very little runway is needed.

AT TOUCHDOWN, POWER OFF, FLAPS UP, APPLY BREAKS

Besides powering off, flaps up eliminates that little lift that we discussed earlier. For the shortest possible landing, apply brakes.

Photo by James Spudich

A graceful aircraft is one of the most elegant examples of human ingenuity

Chapter 3
Create Other Personal Checklists & Flight Charts

In addition to the written checklist for examining the intactness of your airplane and its basic functionality, which is absolutely essential for safety, there are many other checklists and charts that you can devise that enhance your safety margin considerably and simply increase your joy of flying. In this chapter, I describe charts that I have created over the years that deal with following the progress of my flight, V-speeds and performance specifications for each airplane I fly, RPM and manifold pressure (MP) settings for straight and level flight as well as for descents at particular airspeeds, and, importantly, for engine failure emergencies. There are many other areas of flying where creating such personalized charts can be rewarding, but those described here should serve my intended purpose of setting you on the right track of creating your own.

Your Personal Progress of Flight Chart

Remember that organization in the cockpit is essential to safety. You should be in the habit of writing down all important information regarding your flight. Many pilots write such information onto a blank pad – that's better than nothing. But there are crucial pieces of information that I like to have in the same place on my pad for every flight, for quick referral (Fig. 3).

I created this chart as a Word file. Modify it as you see fit and make your own! When I print out this file, it measures 5.2 x 8.7 inches and neatly fits onto the clipboard of, for example, the Harper Aviation Ultimate Kneeboard.

At the top I have spaces for the all important issue of fuel burn rate. I fly the Pipers a lot, where you must switch manually between the right and left fuel tanks. I therefore show both the left and right tanks on my Progress of Flight Chart.

When tanks are full, I always start with the left tank. I record the time on the left tank, fly for 30 minutes (**min**) and then record the time switching to the right tank. Then I switch tanks every 60 min.

Just below the fuel information, I have space for the details of the flight plan that I filed. Just flying around burning holes in the sky is fun, but maximum safety means that you filed either a VFR or IFR flight plan. Why have that on a second piece of paper that you have to fumble for? The order shown is the standard flight plan order of information to give to a briefer.

Below the flight plan information, I have a shaded space for writing down ATIS information, the first one for the departure airport, in the order of the ATIS as you hear it. The information code goes at the far right, under **Info**. After recording the altimeter (**altim**) setting, I set the altimeter and record the difference (**altΔ**) between the actual altitude of my spot on the airport and the altitude indicated on the altimeter. I note the actual time of departure (**atd**) upon takeoff. The second ATIS block is for writing down the ATIS information as I approach my destination airport. After landing, I record here my actual time of arrival (**ata**).

Just below the ATIS boxes, I record important information about the plane's performance for that flight. While in cruise flight, I check that the performance of my plane is as expected with respect to the cylinder head temperature (**CHT**), exhaust gas temperature (**EGT**), gallons per hour (**GPH**) being consumed, and indicated airspeed (**IAS**) for the particular altitude (**ALT**) and manifold pressure (**MP**) and **RPM** settings that I am using. Checking that all of these numbers are similar to what I usually get and that they correspond closely to those described in the pilot operating handbook (POH) for that airplane tells me a lot about whether something is amiss. I want to know this when things are first going wrong rather than when I have a full blown engine problem or some other device problem.

Finally, I need space for the clearance information given to me by the controller. I will always be cleared (**Cl**) to somewhere and finally told to maintain (**M**) a particular altitude and to use a departure frequency (**DF**) and to squawk (**SQ**) a particular transponder code, usually in that order. I have plenty of space below that information to copy other clearances or information during the flight.

As I move from sector to sector, I write down the changes in frequencies (**Freq**) and changes in altitude (**Alt**) given to me by the controller. I find that it works well to have a column for these frequency and altitude changes running down the right side of my sheet. I keep changing and evolving my organization sheet, but the version shown in Fig. 3 works well. You should create one that suits your own personal needs.

Date		From				To		
	Left Fuel				**Right Fuel**			
	time on		min used		time on		min used	

VFR/IFR N   type   kts   dep apt   dep time   alt

Route

dest   ete   hrs fuel   alter apt   name/apt/ph #abd   color

apt	time	wind		wx			Info
T/D	altim	apch		rwy	alt Δ	atd	

ALT   MP   RPM   CHT#   EGT#   GPH   IAS

apt	time	wind		wx			Info
T/D	altim	apch		rwy	alt Δ	ata	

CI

	Freq	Alt
M DF SQ		

Fig. 3. Progress of Flight Chart

Upper photo by John Mercer
Lower photo by James Spudich

Flying in VFR conditions is pure joy - flying in IFR conditions is total satisfaction

V-Speeds and Performance Specifications for the Airplanes you Fly

In thinking further about organization in the cockpit, another chart that I find useful to have in my nav-data kneeboard is a list of the V-speeds and the Performance Specs for the various airplanes I fly. In the example shown in Fig. 4, three airplanes are documented on one page. The Warriors and Skyhawks are simpler of course, but you can use the format shown to set up charts for yourself for whatever airplanes you fly. Customize your charts. Make them personal. Mine are only examples.

It helps to group things into subcategories. Thus, the rotation speed (Vr), maximum angle of climb speed (Vx), maximum rate of climb speed (Vy), and stall speed clean (Vs) all deal with critical issues upon takeoff. The best glide speed, the enroute climb speed, the maneuvering speed (Va), maximum structural cruise speed (Vno), never exceed speed (Vne), and the maximum windows open speed (Vwo) all deal with cruise flight primarily. My third grouping deals primarily with the landing phase of flight: the maximum speed for lowering the gear (Vlo), the maximum speed with the gear down (Vle), the maximum speeds for lowering the flaps (Vfe), the stall speed in landing configuration (Vso), and the maximum demonstrated cross wind landing (Vcw). Clearly all of the V-speeds are relevant to all phases of flight, but I still find this grouping to be helpful.

Certain performance specifications are also useful to have in front of you. Takeoff ground roll distance is shown in Fig. 4 without and with a 50-ft obstacle to deal with. The same is true for the landing ground roll. Remember that the worst-case scenario is different from these values obtained from the airplane's manual. The dependence of these numbers on altitude, temperature and moisture must not be forgotten. High, hot and humid will drive these numbers to much higher values. And the 2.75 quarts of oil as a minimum for the Dakota, as taken from the POH, is truly an absolute minimum that you would not allow your airplane to reach.

V-SPEEDS	KIAS	Cutlass C172RG II/A	Skylane C182/A	Dakota PA28-236/G
	Vr	55	50	60 - 65
SL - 100	Vx	67 - 68	54 - 62	73
SL - 100	Vy	84 - 77	78 - 72	85
stall spd, flps up	Vs	50	48	65
hvy-lt	Best Glide	73 - 61	70	85
	Enroute Climb	85 - 95	78	100
hvy-lt	Va	106 - 89	111 - 89	124 - 96
max struc cruise	Vno	145	143	137
	Vne	164	179	173
max windows open	Vwo	164	179	
max gear extnd spd	Vlo	140		
max spd gear dwn	Vle	164		
first 10°	Vfe	130	140	102
> 10°	Vfe	100	95	102
stall spd, ldg config	Vso	42	45	56
max dem x wind	Vcw	15	15	17
PERFORMANCE SPECS				
Max T/O or Ldg Wt		2,650	2,950	3,000
Max Ramp Wt		2,658	2,960	3,011
Basic Empty Wt		1,598	1,824	1,776
Max Useful Load		1,060	1,136	1,235
Max Baggage		200	200	200
T/O Ground roll		1060/ 1775	705/ 1350	900/ 1100
Rate Climb S.L.		800	1,010	1,100
Cruise, 75% @ 8000		138	144	142
EGT Rich of Peak		50° F	50° F	50° F
Service Ceiling		16,800	16,500	16,000
Landing Ground Roll		625/ 1340	590/ 1350	820/ 1720
Total Fuel		66 gal	92 gal	77 gal
Useable Fuel		62 gal	88 gal	72 gal
Oil, Sump		8 qts	12 qts	12 qts
Oil, Minimum		5 qts	9 qts	2.75 qts
BHP		180 @2700	230 @2400	235 @2400

Fig. 4. V-Speeds and Performance Specifications
(Not to be used without verification of information from official sources)

Regarding the grouping for the performance specifications, the first group relates primarily to takeoff, the second group to cruise, and the third to landing. The fourth group, fuel, oil and horsepower information, relate to all phases of flight. You don't want to takeoff, cruise, or land with too little fuel! Again, all information is actually important for all phases of flight, but the groupings shown have some basis that I personally find useful.

One thing I find convenient about having multiple airplanes on one page is to see how the numbers vary from one plane to another. Many of the numbers are similar for many single-engine aircraft, but notice for example that while the Cutlass and the Skylane have similar best glide speeds, the best glide speed for the Dakota is 10 to 15 KIAS faster.

Notice that Vx and Vy depend on the altitude to some degree. Vx goes up slightly with increased altitude while Vy goes down more appreciably (sea level and 10,000 feet MSL are shown). The best maneuvering speed, Va, depends on how heavy the airplane is. Heavier means higher values of Va.

You may wish to add or subtract from this chart, or make one in a totally different format. The point is, if you make charts of the types that I describe here, you not only have critical information at your fingertips while flying, but you learn new things or remind yourself of things you once learned but have since forgotten.

Customize your charts. Make them personal. Mine are only examples.

RPM or MP Settings and Descent Rates

Let us assume that you want to cruise at 116 KIAS in your C172. What power setting do you need for straight and level flight at 116 KIAS? You are 40 miles out from your destination and you decide to start a 500-fpm descent at 20 miles out (see Chapter 4 for a convenient and simple calculation for making this decision). What power setting will give you your 500-fpm descent at 116 KIAS? Wouldn't it be nice to know such power setting numbers for each airplane you fly. You then back off on the power to that setting and let the plane settle into its descent, at 116 KIAS, without fiddling each time to find the right power setting. This is the professional way to do it, and your passengers will enjoy the smoothness of your transitions.

Again, organization charts are so important for all aspects of flight. This is no exception. My chart for the Cessna Skyhawk (C172) is shown in Fig. 5A.

The Skyhawk is simple because it is not a high performance or complex airplane and one only needs to deal with RPM settings. Assume you are at full throttle. It is apparent from the upper half of the chart in Fig. 5A that cruise at 4000 MSL at 116 KIAS needs a prop setting of about 2600 RPM. To achieve a 500-fpm descent at the same speed, simply reduce the RPM to 2300. No trim adjustment is necessary. If you wish to descend a bit faster (125 fpm), then set the RPM at 2400 and adjust the trim a bit forward.

This chart is particularly useful if you are flying IFR and getting ready to fly an instrument approach. Having at your fingertips the RPM settings that are relevant for a 500-fpm precision approach and a 750-fpm nonprecision approach makes things go much smoother. I fly my approaches at 100 KIAS with no flaps, and I want these RPM settings to be particularly apparent on my charts. Hence, I've boxed in these areas on my chart to highlight these important values. If I want to shoot the approach slower and with 20° flaps, I have those settings on the chart as well.

CESSNA SKYHAWK C172			160 HP@2700		
CONFIGURATION	**RPM** (in)	**VSI** (fpm)	**IAS** (KIAS)	**FLAPS**	**FUEL** (gph)
TAKEOFF, CRUISE & DESCENT					
Climb S.L., 2300#, 15°C	2500	500	85	up	
Max Rate Climb S.L., 2300#, 15°C	full fwd	645	78	up	
Cruise 4000', 2300#, 61% BHP, 7°C	2400	0	106	up	6.9
Cruise 4000', 2300#, 75% BHP, 7°C	2600	0	116	up	8.3
Cruise Descent, pwr Δ 4000', 2300#, 75% BHP, 7°C	2300	500	116	up	
Cruise Descent, pitch dwn Δ 4000', 2300#, 61% BHP, 7°C	2400	500	125	up	
	RPM	**VSI** (fpm)	**IAS** (KIAS)	**FLAPS**	**FUEL** (gph)
IFR APPROACHES					
Approach Level Flt 4000', 2300#, 7°C	2300	0	100	up	
Precision Approach Descent from 4000', 2300#, 7°C	2000	500	100	up	
Non-precision Approach Descent from 4000', 2300#, 7°C	1700	750	100	up	
	RPM	**VSI** (fpm)	**IAS** (KIAS)	**FLAPS**	**FUEL** (gph)
IFR APPROACHES					
Approach Level Flt 4000', 2300#, 7°C	2400	0	80	20°	
Precision Approach Descent from 4000', 2300#, 7°C	1900	500	80	20°	
Non-precision Approach Descent from 4000', 2300#, 7°C	1700	750	80	20°	

Fig. 5A. RPM Settings for Straight and Level Flights and Descents for Particular Airspeeds for a Skyhawk C172
  (Not to be used without verification of information from official sources)

PIPER DAKOTA PA28-236 235 HP@2400						
CONFIGURATION	MP (in)	VSI (fpm)	IAS (KIAS)	FLAPS	RPM	FUEL (gph)
TAKEOFF, CRUISE & DESCENT						
Climb >500', S.L., 2950#, 15°C	25	1000	90	up	2500	
Max Rate Climb >500', S.L., 2950#, 15°C	full fwd	1050	85	up	2400	
Cruise 4000', 2950#, 65% BHP, 7°C	21	0	124	up	2300	11.8
Cruise 4000', 2950#, 75% BHP, 7°C	23	0	134	up	2300	13.6
Cruise Descent, pwr Δ 4000', 2950#, 76% BHP, 7°C	17	500	120	up	2300	
Cruise Descent, pitch dwn Δ 4000', 2950#, 68% BHP, 7°C	23	500	137	up	2300	
	MP (in)	VSI (fpm)	IAS (KIAS)	FLAPS	RPM	FUEL (gph)
IFR APPROACHES						
Approach Level Flt 4000', 2950#, 7°C	17	0	100	up	full fwd	
Precision Approach Descent from 4000', 2950#, 7°C	14	500	100	up	full fwd	
Non-precision Approach Descent from 4000', 2950#, 7°C	12	750	100	up	full fwd	
	MP (in)	VSI (fpm)	IAS (KIAS)	FLAPS	RPM	FUEL (gph)
IFR APPROACHES						
Approach Level Flt 4000', 2950#, 7°C	16	0	90	up	full fwd	
Precision Approach Descent from 4000', 2950#, 7°C	13	500	90	up	full fwd	
Non-precision Approach Descent from 4000', 2950#, 7°C	11	750	90	up	full fwd	

Fig. 5B. MP Settings for Straight and Level Flights and Descents for Particular Airspeeds for a Piper Dakota
  (Not to be used without verification of information from official sources)

Fig. 5B shows a similar chart for the Piper Dakota, which is more complex since it has a constant-speed propeller. Now the MP is the important setting to have fixed in mind. But all the same issues described for the Cessna 172 above apply, and I use the chart for the Dakota in essentially the same way.

Remember, your charts are highly personal. You may well choose to emphasize different airspeeds, different descent rates, or other parameters associated with your cruise and descents. The point is it's your chart. Make it what you want it to be.

Having at your fingertips the RPM settings that are relevant for a 500-fpm precision approach and a 750-fpm nonprecision approach makes things go much smoother

Chapter 4
Cockpit Tips

Climbs and Descents

How Far from Your Destination You Should Start Your Descent

You have been taught to keep your passengers comfortable by restricting your turns to standard rate or less, and to climb or descend at no more than 500 fpm. In order to comply with these comfort margins, there are some simple things you can do instead of just "winging it." The bank angles on turns are no problem, and climbs are easily managed so as not to be too steep. Descents, on the other hand, are another matter.

How many times have you been flying to an airport of choice and neglected to start your descent early enough to be able to keep your descent rate at 500 fpm? How can you decide when to begin a descent (Fig. 6)? I describe on the next page a simple rule to use.

A good airspeed as you near your destination is about 100-120 KIAS (The ground speed is what really counts of course, but I will use KIAS here as an approximation that works pretty well).

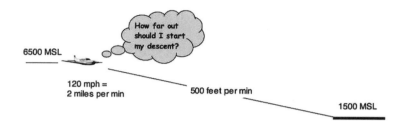

Fig. 6. Distance Out to Start a Descent

A simple rule to estimate how many miles (that is, nautical miles) out you should start your descent is:

1. determine the altitude that you need to lose (your MSL altitude minus the MSL elevation of the airport, which you always want to determine before getting near the airport anyway)
2. *divide that number by 1000,* and then
3. *multiply that number by 4.*

The resultant is the miles out from the airport that you should start your descent. This simple rule derives from the following calculations. Let's say you are at 6500 MSL and the airport elevation is 1500 MSL, as in Fig. 6. Then the time to the airport is

(6500 -1500) ft / 500 fpm = 10 min to the airport.

A descent speed of 120 mph corresponds to 2 miles per minute. Thus,

$$\frac{(6500\text{-}1500) \text{ ft}}{500 \text{ ft per min}} \text{ X } 2 \text{ miles per min} = \text{ the miles out to begin your descent}$$

Instead of dividing the altitude you need to lose by 500 and multiplying by 2, it's easier to divide by 1000 and multiply by 4. Thus, in the case presented, you must lose 5000 ft, so you should begin your descent at 20 miles out. If you had to lose 9000 ft, it would be 36 miles out, and so forth.

If you are flying into an uncontrolled airport and want to fly overhead at 2000 feet AGL, then you would level off at 3500 MSL in the example given and have your 2000 feet AGL stabilized for your airport flyover.

Thanks to André Bennett for pointing out this simple rule to me on a great flight in 1995 from Palo Alto across the Sierras and Rockies to St. Louis in N9505P, a Comanche 260C that I shared ownership of with my friends and colleagues Heinz Furthmayr and Uta Francke.

Once you have decided how far out to begin your descent, what is the RPM setting (or MP setting for an airplane with a constant speed propeller) on the airplane that you fly that will be close to what you need for a 500-fpm descent? Just look at the chart you created for yourself in Chapter 3, which is right in front of you on your kneepad.

> ## To estimate how many miles out to start your descent, divide the altitude you need to lose by 1000 and multiply that number by 4

Organization of Your Kneeboard

You have now created your personal versions of all of the charts and checklists described in Chapters 1 and 3, as well as others that you find useful but not described there. Where do you keep them? A highly organized kneeboard is a welcomed commodity, especially when you get into somewhat tight situations and you want to get your hands on the relevant materials quickly.

My first page, front side, in my 7-ring kneeboard shows the main points to follow in the event of engine failure (Fig. 7A).

ENGINE FAILURE

1. BEST GLIDE

Best Glide	**85**	Dakota
Best Glide	**70**	C182 & C172RG
Trim		set

2. TOWARD BEST FIELD INTO WIND

3. FUEL PUMP ON, CHANGE TANKS

IF ENOUGH ALTITUDE (>3000 FT):

4. TROUBLE SHOOT

Mixture	rich & lean
Props	move, then full forward
Throttle	pump
Carb Heat	on
Primer	in & locked
Magnetos	cycle, keep on best
Master	on

5. COMMUNICATE

SQ	7700
Frequency	current or 121.5
Talk	report posn, #on board, fuel

6. SECURE AIRCRAFT & LAND

Fuel Valve	to off
Mixture	idle cutoff
Ignition	off
Master	off
Gear	as required
Doors	unlatch before touchdown

Fig. 7A. Chart Concerning Engine Failure Emergencies
(Not to be used without verification of information from official sources)

The back side of the first page of my kneeboard shows a diagram emphasizing the best way to approach a landing that is destined to be a power off landing (Fig. 7B). I also have room on the back for a list of local airports, their relevant frequencies, and their pattern altitudes in feet MSL.

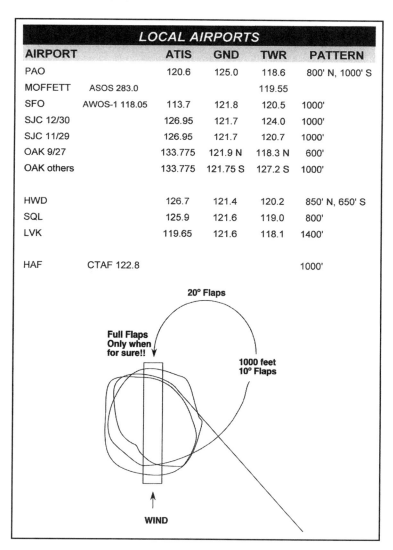

AIRPORT		ATIS	GND	TWR	PATTERN
PAO		120.6	125.0	118.6	800' N, 1000' S
MOFFETT	ASOS 283.0			119.55	
SFO	AWOS-1 118.05	113.7	121.8	120.5	1000'
SJC 12/30		126.95	121.7	124.0	1000'
SJC 11/29		126.95	121.7	120.7	1000'
OAK 9/27		133.775	121.9 N	118.3 N	600'
OAK others		133.775	121.75 S	127.2 S	1000'
HWD		126.7	121.4	120.2	850' N, 650' S
SQL		125.9	121.6	119.0	800'
LVK		119.65	121.6	118.1	1400'
HAF	CTAF 122.8				1000'

Fig. 7B. Chart and Graph Concerning Engine Failure Emergencies and Local Airport Information
(Not to be used without verification of information from official sources)

Some instructors teach to circle on the right side of your landing stretch, rather than over it as shown in Fig. 7B, with turns to the left so you can always keep the landing stretch in site. Also, whether you add 20° of flaps on your base leg turn, as shown in Fig. 7B, depends critically of course on the winds. You have to judge the winds particularly carefully. This is why you should practice power off landings quite often.

If I ever have an engine failure, I want to be able to get to my written checklist. I simply flip to the very first page of my kneeboard. Having said that, clearly the items on the emergency checklist should be "memory items." Your priority is to fly the airplane. Once you are settled into the emergency landing procedure, you may have time to revert to the checklist.

My next 7-hole plastic holder in my kneeboard holds the 3,4 Jeppesen Low Altitude Enroute Charts, the Jeppesen San Francisco Area Chart for IFR, a Jeppesen IFR enroute plotter, and a combination sec-wac-tac ruler for VFR charts. The next plastic holder in my kneepad has the IFR approach charts for Palo Alto airport, the airport that I fly out of. I insert other charts into this part of my kneeboard before going on a trip, depending on the route and destination. The other charts and graphs that I have on my kneeboard are those depicted in Chapters 1, 2 and 3 of this book. Several pens and pencils are, of course, attached to the kneeboard for ready access.

Clearly the items on the emergency checklist should be "memory items." Your priority is to fly the airplane. Once you are settled into the emergency landing procedure, you may have time to revert to the checklist.

Organization of Your Flight Bag

Your flight bag must be well organized and readily accessible during your flight. You can get away with a lot of disorganization if nothing ever goes wrong and you always fly VFR. But you will really appreciate your efforts to be organized when things don't go so smoothly, especially if you are in instrument meteorological conditions (IMC). Fig. 8 shows the organization of my flight bag.

In the front flap of my main bag, I keep two flashlights, extra pencils and pens, a Denalt time / speed /distance computer, a dipstick for checking my avgas level,

Fig. 8. Organization of Flight Bag. Upper left: front flap and side pockets of flight bag. Middle right: main compartment and back pockets. Lower left: headset bag.

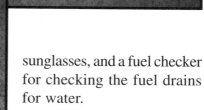

sunglasses, and a fuel checker for checking the fuel drains for water.

In the left pocket of my main bag I carry extra AA and AAA batteries, motion sickness bags, ear plugs for passengers, an all purpose survival tool, two failed instrument covers, and a stop watch attached to a yoke holder.

In the pocket on the right, I carry my transceiver hand-held nav/com, an extra battery pack for the transceiver, and an adapter that connects it to my headsets. In my thirty years of flying, I have lost all my electrical equipment twice, once at night leaving me in complete darkness. Sure, I could have managed by waving wings and following light signals, but there is no way that I would fly without a good hand-held nav/com. I had one with me for both of my experiences with electrical failures, and the result was that both situations were managed with ease. Being able to communicate and navigate on a battery operated device (with an extra battery pack and extra loose batteries always in my bag) is great insurance. And we are only talking about a couple of hundred dollars! That's about two hours of flying time. So do yourself a favor and invest in one of these early in your flying career.

The main compartment of my bag is split with a divider. In the smaller section I keep my Garmin GPSMAP 196, already attached to its yoke attachment. I have not always had a GPS unit in my bag, but now I am spoiled and there is no way that I would fly without it. The situational awareness it provides is really wonderful and, when used correctly, it is a terrific addition to safety. Chapter 6 deals with GPS in some detail.

In the larger part of the main compartment, I carry my logbook, Jeppesen Airway Manual, the Pilots Guide to California Airports, the Southwest U.S. Airport/Facility Directory, and my Harper Aviation Ultimate Kneeboard, which has seven rings and holds the Jeppesen 7-ring sheet protectors carrying the charts and checklists described in Chapters 1, 2 and 3.

The outer compartment on the back of my flight bag holds various Sectional Charts, VFR Terminal Area Charts, and other general informational items like the VFR-IFR information card from King Schools, Inc.

My headset bag holds two headsets. One is a Peltor, which folds up and therefore takes very little room. Extra pens, pencils and another flashlight are kept in the headset bag outer compartments.

Photo by John Mercer

Imagine flying over mountains of the Continental Divide with a friend to fly fish on a remote river in total solitude

Photos by James Spudich

Only from the cockpit of a small plane can one experience the true drama of the vast uninhabited spaces of the American Southwest

Chapter 5
Weight and Balance

Consequences of Not Being within the Center of Gravity Envelopes

How often do you check the weight and balance of your airplane before departure? Many pilots check weight and balance for their checkride and not often after that, even though they are loading up a plane full of passengers with a full tank of gas! As driven home to me by Avram Goldstein, a friend and early instructor of mine and author of several terrific books on flying, if you try this in a Cessna 172, your airplane will definitely be overweight (unless you have very small passengers).

What if you are not within the center of gravity (CG) envelopes? Will you be able to physically takeoff? Probably yes. But is it safe? Absolutely not!

If you are too heavy, then the biggest danger, assuming you have a long enough runway for the increased takeoff roll that will be needed, is that you will totally stress your airplane beyond its limits in a steep turn or by encountering turbulence, where the G forces are such that the weight of the airplane goes up considerably. Losing a part of the airplane is a very real possibility.

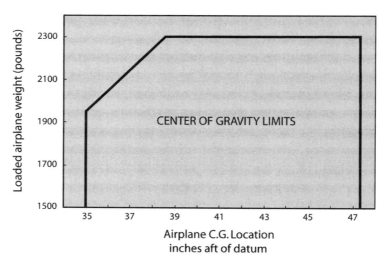

Fig. 9. A center of gravity limits graph for the Cessna 172
Modified version of that appearing in the Cessna 172 POH.

What if you are not overweight, but out of limits aft (to the right of the limits illustrated in Fig. 9; weight distribution too far to the rear)? *This scenario is clearly the very worst one.* You may be able to get off the ground with your yoke full forward, but getting your nose down to recover from a stall while in the air may be nearly impossible.

If you are out of limits forward (to the left of the limits illustrated in Fig. 9; weight distribution too far to the front of the airplane), you may have a serious problem landing (assuming you can get off the ground in the first place by holding the yoke in the full back position). If you can't flare properly on landing, you are likely to dig your prop right into the ground.

Weight and Balance, an Easy Way

Given the importance of weight and balance, it clearly makes sense to have an easy way to make sure you are within limits every time you fly. Let's take a closer look at the Cessna 172, using typical generic values found in the Pilot Operating Handbook (POH).

The basic empty weight will clearly be different for each Cessna 172. Let's assume this one has a basic empty weight of 1454.0 lbs. The chart in Fig. 10 shows an Excel sheet with weight and balance for that airplane. A Cessna 172 Skyhawk with standard full tanks can carry some weight in the baggage area, a pilot and copilot with a combined weight of 340 lbs, but then no more than 170 lbs of passenger in the back seat.

WEIGHT & BALANCE SKYHAWK C172	gal	lbs/ gal	Weight lbs	Arm Aft Datum inches	Moment in-lbs /1000
Basic Empty Weight			1454.0	39.6	57.6
Pilot & Front Passenger			340.0	37.0	12.6
Passengers Rear Seat			170.0	73.0	12.4
Useable Fuel (38 gal max)	38.0	6.0	228.0	48.0	10.9
Baggage Area 1 (120 lbs)*			100.0	95.0	9.5
Baggage Area 2 (50 lbs max)*			15.0	123	1.8
Ramp Weight (2307 lbs max)			2307.0	45.5	104.9
Fuel Allowance (Start/Taxi/Runup)			-7.0	48.0	-0.3
Takeoff Weight (2300 lbs max)			2300.0	45.4	104.5
*max combined weight in Baggage Areas 1 and 2 = 120 lbs					

Fig. 10. A Simple Weight and Balance Spreadsheet for a Cessna 172 Skyhawk

(Not to be used without verification of information from official sources)

To make the weight and balance easier to check, make an Excel spreadsheet on your computer (Fig. 10). While this chapter is a bit on the technical side, if you have not had much experience using an Excel program, this is an excellent time to become acquainted with it. It is not difficult and the payoff is big.

Since Fig. 10 is an Excel spreadsheet, and if you have it on your computer, the numbers in the grey spaces, call cells, are the only ones you need to change from one flight to another. The rest will be calculated automatically for you using the fixed numbers or formulas (see below) that you put into the appropriate cells in the Excel sheet. Thus, you need to enter:

√   the actual Basic Empty Weight of the particular C172 that you are flying (*from the weight and balance data in that particular airplane*)
√   the weights of the front and rear seat occupants
√   the gal of useable fuel in the airplane
√   and the weight in the two baggage areas.

The Arm Aft Datum cells are fixed numbers for a C172, except for the Ramp Weight row and the Takeoff Weight row. All of the other cells are either products or sums of various sorts. Thus, the top six cells in the far right column are the products of the respective Weights and Arm Aft Datum of those rows, divided by 1000. The fourth row value under the Weight column is calculated by multiplying the number of useable gallons of fuel on board by 6.0 lbs/gal. The weights are summed in the row labeled Ramp Weight, as are the Moments. The Arm Aft Datum of that row is then obtained as a product of 1000 x Moment x (1/Weight) of that row. The fuel allowance upon startup, taxi and runup then serves as a correction for the final total Takeoff Weight, Arm Aft Datum, and Moment, shown in the last row. Again, the Arm Aft Datum is a product of 1000 x Moment x (1/Weight) of that row. These three values are then checked against the graphs showing the Center of Gravity Limits (Fig. 9) and the Center of Gravity Moment Envelope. These graphs can be scanned into your excel file for ready access.

Do you have a Personal Digital Assistant (PDA)? If so, here is a bonus feature that you may be able to use. My PDA allows me to import my Excel file into its "Document to Go" folder. I can then do the weight and balance check on my PDA by filling in the numbers in the grey cells and getting an automatic readout of my final Takeoff Weight, Arm Aft Datum, and Moment. This is extremely convenient. Otherwise, you can use a calculator and do the math yourself using the fixed numbers in the grey cells and the table as a guide.

Weight and Balance, the Easiest Way

I now describe a more elegant way to set up your Excel spreadsheet for your weight and balance calculation. This method is simply an extension of the previous Excel sheet. The most convenient thing to do is to calculate into the Excel sheet the CG envelope that is relevant to the particular airplane you fly. That is, you basically put the relevant CG envelope, such as the one shown in Fig. 9, into the Excel program itself. This way you can have your computer automatically check whether you are within the limits of the envelope and then tell you whether it is **OK** to go or it is a **NO GO** for any of the possible weight or center of gravity (CG) considerations. The trick is coming up with the correct formula to describe the relevant envelope for the CG and weight limits. Again, while this is a fairly technical chapter, working through it is highly worth while.

In the Cessna 182 Skylane example shown in Fig. 11, the fuel tanks are full with 88 gal usable fuel, and the weights for the pilot, passengers and baggage are as shown, in lbs. These values were entered into the grey boxes in B2 (column B, row 2) and B4 through B7. Onetime entries particular to the Skylane were entered for the basic empty weight and its total moment (light grey boxes; B9 and E9, respectively).

The other onetime entries for the particular airplane you fly are basically a mathematical description of the center of gravity limits graph from the Pilot Operating Handbook. A graph for the Skylane is shown in Fig. 12. The entries describing this graph are all shown in the light grey boxes in I3 through I8. These are the maximum and minimum take off (T/O) weights, the minimum and maximum CG values, and the CG curve weight. This latter number is the point on the CG limits envelope where the curve breaks (CG 33 and 2250 loaded weight).

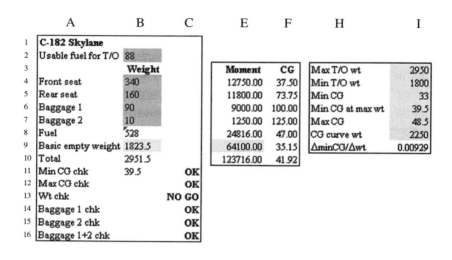

Fig. 11. Weight and balance for a Cessna 182 Skylane
  (Not to be used without verification of information from official sources)

Once you have made those entries, everything else in Fig. 11 is calculated and you get an immediate **OK** or **NO GO** readout in C11 through C16 for the CG limits and weight checks. In the case shown, all is **OK** except for the total weight check (Wt chk, C13), which is a **NO GO** because the total weight of the airplane is 2951.5 lbs (B10) and the maximum takeoff weight is 2950 lbs (I3).

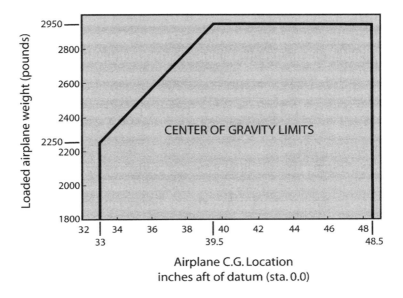

Fig. 12. A center of gravity limits graph for a Cessna 182
Modified version of that appearing in the Cessna 182 POH.

Photo by James Spudich

Big or small, your weight and balance must be within limits

The formulas for the various calculations are shown in the following figures, which refer to the right, middle and left boxes of Fig. 11.

	H	I
3	Max T/O wt	2950
4	Min T/O wt	1800
5	Min CG	33
6	Min CG at max wt	39.5
7	Max CG	48.5
8	CG curve wt	2250
9	ΔminCG/Δwt	=(I6-I5)/(I3-I8)

Fig. 13. Formulas for the box on the right of Fig. 11
(Not to be used without verification of information from official sources)

The formula in I9, Fig. 13, relates the change in minimum CG (ΔminCG) as a function of the change in weight (Δwt) between CG locations 33 and 39.5 (see Fig. 12). Thus, the total curve is defined by the values in the right box of Fig. 11.

	E	F
	Moment	**CG**
3		
4	=B4*37.5	=IF(B4=0,0,E4/B4)
5	=B5*73.75	=IF(B5=0,0,E5/B5)
6	=B6*100	=IF(B6=0,0,E6/B6)
7	=B7*125	=IF(B7=0,0,E7/B7)
8	=B8*47	=IF(B8=0,0,E8/B8)
9	64100	=IF(B9=0,0,E9/B9)
10	=SUM(E4:E9)	=IF(B10=0,0,E10/B10)

Fig. 14. Formulas for the box in the middle of Fig. 11
(Not to be used without verification of information from official sources)

The formulas in column E of Fig. 14 calculate the moments for the respective weights entered in column B of the left box of Fig. 11. The formulas in column F calculate the CG values for the respective weights entered in column B of the left box of Fig. 11. These values are set to 0 if the weight is 0, otherwise the CG is the moment divided by the weight.

	A	B	C
1	C-182 Skylane		
2	Usable fuel for T/O	88	
3		**Weight**	
4	Front seat	340	
5	Rear seat	160	
6	Baggage 1	90	
7	Baggage 2	10	
8	Fuel	=B2*6	
9	Basic empty weight	1823.5	
10	Total	=SUM(B4:B9)	
11	Min CG chk	=IF(B10<I8,I5,I5+(B10-I8)*I9)	=IF(F10<B11,"NO GO","OK")
12	Max CG chk		=IF(F10>I7,"NO GO","OK")
13	Wt chk		=IF(B10<I4,"NO GO",IF(B10>I3,"NO GO","OK"))
14	Baggage 1 chk		=IF(B6>200,"NO GO","OK")
15	Baggage 2 chk		=IF(B7>80,"NO GO","OK")
16	Baggage 1+2 chk		=IF(B6+B7>200,"NO GO","OK")

Fig. 15. Formulas for the box on the left of Fig. 11

(Not to be used without verification of information from official sources)

The formula in B8 of Fig. 15 calculates the weight of the fuel in lbs, given the gallons of fuel entered into B2. The total weight of the loaded airplane (B10) is the sum of B4 through B9.

The minimum CG check (Min CG chk, see row 11 of Fig. 11 and Fig. 15) is complicated by the fact that the minimum CG depends on the weight of the airplane (see Center of Gravity Limits graph, Fig. 12). Therefore, first the minimum CG for the final weight of the airplane must be calulated. That is accomplished by the formula in B11, Fig. 15. Then the formula in C11 tests whether F10<B11 (to the left of the limits illustrated in Fig. 12). If so, it is a **NO GO** (CG is out of limits forward; i.e., the weight distribution is too far to the front of the airplane), otherwise it is **OK**. The formula in C12 tests whether the maximum CG limit is exceeded (to the right of the limits illustrated in Fig. 12). If so, it is a **NO GO** (CG is out

of limits aft; the weight distribution is too far to the rear), otherwise it is **OK**. The formulas in C13 through C16 test whether any of the weights have been exceeded.

What about the same type of Excel spreadsheet for the Piper Dakota? This one is complicated only by the fact that the Weight versus CG Envelope graph changes slope once upon reaching 1900 lbs total airplane weight and then again at 2500 lbs. The formula for the minimum CG as a function of total weight is therefore more complex. Now you have a Min CG_1, a Min CG_2, a CG curve wt_1, a CG curve wt_2, a $\Delta minCG/\Delta wt_1$ and a $\Delta minCG/\Delta wt_2$. Thus, examination of the Dakota chart in Fig. 16 shows that the formula in B11, Fig. 15 becomes:

$$=IF(B10<=1900,79.8,IF(B10<=2500,79.8+(B10-1900)*0.0045,82.5+(B10-2500)*0.012)).$$

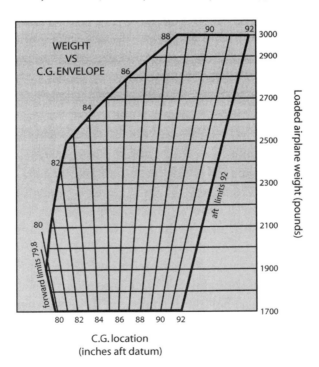

Fig. 16. A weight versus center of gravity envelope for the Piper Dakota. Modified version of that appearing in the Dakota POH.

That is,

- √ If the total weight of the airplane is less than or equal to 1900 lbs, then the minimum CG location is 79.8.
- √ If the total weight is less than or equal to 2500 lbs, then the minimum CG location is 79.8 + (total weight - 1900) x (ΔminCG/Δwt$_1$, for the curve between 1900 and 2500 lbs).
- √ Otherwise, the minimum CG location is 82.5 + (total weight - 2500) x (ΔminCG/Δwt$_2$, for the curve between 2500 and 3000 lbs).

If you have a PDA and can load the weight and balance Excel files for each airplane you fly into it, you can then enter the various weight numbers before each flight and get an instantaneous readout of whether you are **NO GO** in any category!

While this chapter is a bit technical, given the importance of accurate weight and balance considerations, I have found the approaches described here to be extremely useful for ready access to whether I am within my limitations of weight and balance before each flight. If you are not inclined to use the information in this chapter to create an Excel spreadsheet yourself, I would encourage you to find a friend who is familiar with the Excel program and who will create the spreadsheet for you. The goal of this chapter, indeed of the entire book, is to help you be a safer pilot.

Calculate into an Excel sheet the CG envelope that is relevant to the particular airplane you fly. This way you can have your computer automatically check whether you are within the limits of the envelope.

Photo by James Spudich

When piloting a small aircraft, the ever changing vistas excite wonder and lift the spirits

Chapter 6
The Global Positioning System

GPS Will Take Over as the Primary Navigation System

The Global Positioning System (GPS) is extremely powerful, and it's only a matter of time before it takes over as the primary navigation system for all forms of air transportation. A number of airplanes in the flying club that you use already have GPS units installed. It is therefore essential that you familiarize yourself with the basics of GPS. This chapter is designed to supply you with that basic information and to get you started along the road of using GPS equipment.

GPS equipment that has been certified for IFR can most often be used in place of both ADF and DME in operations normally using those instruments, and in most cases ADF and DME instruments don't even have to be installed in the airplane. Do you want to fly direct from one NDB to another 500 miles away? Now you can.

It is important to note that GPS technology can include Receiver Autonomous Integrity Monitoring (RAIM), and this is a must for serious use of GPS when you fly. This means the receiver monitors the integrity of the signals received by the unit to check for corrupted information.

Current GPS approaches are nonprecision. They provide lateral guidance only, like VOR approaches. Standard GPS receivers use signals from 24 different satellites. Those satellites ensure navigation accuracy to within 100 meters. The FAA has been developing a system for better position accuracy using a system of satellites and ground stations that provide GPS signal corrections. This is known as the Wide Area Augmentation System (WAAS). As of July 10, 2003, WAAS has been officially turned on. This system provides precision capabilities that rival those of the current instrument landing system (ILS), and vertical control is now possible if you have a WAAS-enabled GPS receiver in your aircraft.

Basically, WAAS is a network of terrestrial wide area reference stations linked to a special master station to further remove errors in GPS signals. Correction messages are sent to WAAS satellites and from there the signals are relayed to WAAS-enabled GPS receivers in your aircraft. This results in an incredible accuracy of better than 8 meters both laterally and vertically, which is already more than sufficient for highly accurate precision approaches. The opportunities opened by this development are incredible and extend far beyond the ability to shoot precision approaches into essentially any airport of interest. The most important issue is one of safety. Step down fixes and steep descents will be eliminated in place of stabilized descents using glide slope indications for all approaches.

Widespread use of WAAS-enabled GPS will, of course, take some time. The expectation is to certify a few hundred WAAS-enabled GPS approaches per year.

If your airplane has an FAA approved GPS, you can forget about buying all those approach charts and maps, right? Wrong! Computer mapping systems and associated databases *do not* provide all of the navigation information needed for you to conduct a safe and legal flight. Not all instrument flight procedures are coded into a navigational database.

You must understand what your airplane with its GPS system is certified for. If your avionics system is certified for IFR enroute and terminal navigation only, it will not include approaches. If it is certified to fly IFR approaches, it will only include approaches that are authorized when using your particular avionics system.

Stepdown fixes between the Final Approach Fix and the Missed Approach Point are not included in navigational databases. Some categories of controlled airspace are not in your database.

The bottom line is that *you must continue to use your paper charts*. It is critical that all legs of the procedure on the paper chart be flown as charted. If you don't have a paper chart for a particular procedure in your database, you are not authorized to fly it.

Some Basics

With these introductory remarks, let's get down to some of the real basics regarding GPS. For use of GPS equipment, it's important to understand the meanings of heading, bearing, track and desired track. In Fig. 17, the course direction to be flown (128° in this case) from waypoint 1 (WPT1) to waypoint 2 (WPT2) is the direct line connecting those two waypoints, shown by the heavy line in the figure. Upon starting from WPT1, this is clearly your **Desired Track** (DTK). Note that the meaning of DTK is the original course direction that you were to fly between the two waypoints. Thus, 128° is still considered the DTK even if you are off course. The idea is to get back on course and fly the DTK.

Notice that the pilot in Fig. 17 has gotten off course due to two factors: first, she was instructed by ARTCC to fly a **Heading** (HDG, the direction the airplane is pointing) of 113° for traffic avoidance; second, a wind from the Southwest is resulting in a **Track** (TRK, the direction the airplane is going) of 103°. Her distance off track is the **Cross Track Deviation** (CTD). In her present position, the pilot has a **Bearing** (BRG) to the station of 147°. The difference between her TRK and her DTK is the **Track Angle Error** (TAE).

With these definitions clearly understood, the information appearing on your GPS screen is much easier to decipher.

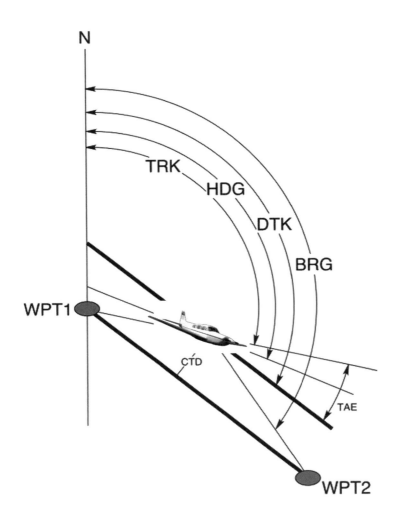

Fig. 17. Diagram illustrating the meaning of track, heading, desired track, bearing, cross track deviation and track angle error

Getting Started with the Garmin GNS 530 Simulator

Let's suppose you rent an airplane that has been outfitted with a Garmin GPS 530. You turn on the Avionics Power Switch and the Garmin GPS comes to life (Fig. 18).

Photo by James Spudich

Fig. 18. The Garmin GNS 530

It is exciting to see your airplane on the moving map, but do you wish you knew more about use of the unit? Instructions and lifelike simulation are readily available as a download from http://www.garmin.com/aviation. If you use a MacIntosh computer, you will need to have the program Virtual PC installed, and you must download the simulation program from within the Windows environment.

The Garmin website page has a box to click on to get the "GNS 530 Simulator." Click on it to initiate the download. The download is a zip file, so you will need to have an unzip utility available on your computer. You can download one for free from the web. After you unzip the Garmin simulator program, go ahead and boot it up. When you finally get the image of the Garmin 530, it will go through a "self test" and then show a blinking "OK?," at which time you should push the **ENT** (for enter) button. You are now operational.

The knobs and push buttons on the left of the simulated Garmin screen are for COM and NAV settings. Those are fairly straightforward to master.

The knobs and buttons on the right of the Garmin screen lead you to tons of information and, for you instrument rated pilots, the ability to shoot approaches and the missed if you need it with ease. I discuss later how to use the Garmin for approaches. For now, it is worth making a card (Fig. 19) to remind you of the four Groups available to you (scroll through the Groups by 'rotating' the large GPS knob on the lower right of the Garmin screen), and the subgroups under each of them (scroll through by 'rotating' the small GPS knob).

The navigation (NAV) group, which you will use the most, includes your heading and compass and the moving map. You can rapidly return to this group no matter where you are within the groups and subgroups by just holding down the **CLR** button.

Once you have selected an airport, the waypoint (WPT) group gives you all the information you could hope for about that airport.

The auxiliary (AUX) group provides flight planning capability.

The nearest (NRST) group not only shows you the nearest airports, but as Fig. 19 shows, it also shows the nearest intersection, NDB, VOR, and others. Just scroll through these using the small GPS knob. Needless to say, the "Nearest Airport" feature is terrific in case of an emergency. Just rotate the large GPS knob fully to the right and you have the information you need.

To get started using the knobs and buttons on the right of the screen, the first thing you should do is to initialize your position at

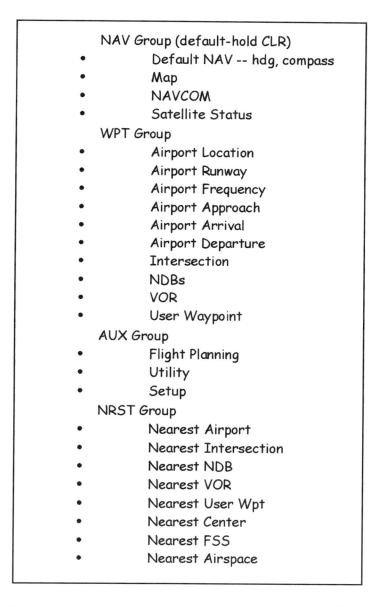

NAV Group (default-hold CLR)
- Default NAV -- hdg, compass
- Map
- NAVCOM
- Satellite Status

WPT Group
- Airport Location
- Airport Runway
- Airport Frequency
- Airport Approach
- Airport Arrival
- Airport Departure
- Intersection
- NDBs
- VOR
- User Waypoint

AUX Group
- Flight Planning
- Utility
- Setup

NRST Group
- Nearest Airport
- Nearest Intersection
- Nearest NDB
- Nearest VOR
- Nearest User Wpt
- Nearest Center
- Nearest FSS
- Nearest Airspace

Fig. 19. Card showing the four main groups for the Garmin 530 and the subgroups under them

your airport of choice, for example Palo Alto. Use the "Options" pull down window and choose "Initialize Position." You enter

"KPAO" in the little window that appears using the small GPS knob to find the letter K and then the large GPS knob to move you to the next space. When you have "KPAO" filled in the space, push the **ENT** button (*the* **ENT** *button is always the way to enter information and to acknowledge questions that pop up on the screen*). Your plane should now be sitting on the Palo Alto airport runway.

How to Fly Directly to an Airport

Here are two ways to fly directly to an airport, VOR, or any other waypoint.

One method to fly direct to a waypoint is:

√ Push the "Direct" button (**D** with an arrow through it) and enter the symbol for your waypoint.
  ■ This is done by rotating the large GPS knob to switch position and the small GPS knob to enter the letter or number of your waypoint, as before. Try entering "KMRY."
√ Once your waypoint is entered, press **ENT** twice to acknowledge the question "activate?" that appears on the Garmin screen.
  ■ A straight magenta line shows the direct path to your destination from where you are. You can change the scale of the map by pushing the up and down triangles on the **RNG** (range) button. By scaling to **150nm-1** (shown on the lower left of the map) you now see Monterey airport.
√ Increase your speed with the speed control knob in the lower part of the figure.
√ Set your HSI to 151°.
  ■ To do this, put your cursor on the yellow arrow knob on the HSI, click on it and hold, and move the cursor to the left and right. If you forget to set your HSI,

you will get a reminder message on the Garmin screen telling you to do so.

√ Now fly the line.
   ■ As you continue your flight, check out information available to you in the other three groups and in all the subgroups. To get back to the NAV group, press the **CLR** button and hold.

The second method to fly direct to a waypoint is:

√ Press the small GPS knob in.
   ■ This highlights an arrow cursor on the screen.
√ Rotate the GPS knobs to move the cursor to the waypoint you want to fly to.
   ■ The waypoint will become highlighted.
√ Press the Direct button.
√ Acknowledge the "activate?" by pressing **ENT** twice.
√ Fly the straight line.

Creating a Flight Plan

One of the great uses of a GPS unit is to set up a flight plan for your route of travel and to be capable of modifying that flight plan quickly and easily while in flight. Using the flight plan feature is wonderful for positional awareness. It is, for example, a great way to avoid boundaries of airspaces that you are not supposed to be in without a clearance.

For VFR flights, you can create your own plan using user waypoints that you establish. On the Garmin GNS 530, the flight plan group consists of two pages, which allow you to create, modify, store, and copy flight plans.

To create and use a flight plan on the Garmin 530:

√ Press the flight plan button (**FPL**) at the bottom of the display.

- ■ Note that for all airports within the United States that have three-letter identifiers (e.g. PAO), one must start with a K (you would use C for Canada and P for Alaska). Thus, you enter KPAO and KSCK if you are flying from Palo Alto to Stockton. Notice that when entering IFR flight plans, Victor airways are not recognized. Thus if you are flying IFR from Palo Alto to Stockton, your flight plan could be KPAO SJC SUNOL ECA KSCK.
- √ Store your flight plan.
  - ■ Once you have created a flight plan, you can store it and then activate it when needed. The Garmin GNS 530 allows one to store up to twenty flight plans.
- √ When ready to take off, activate the flight plan.
- √ Edit your flight plan while enroute.
  - ■ ATC often gives rerouting and therefore you want to become facile with making quick changes on your unit. The instructions on how to do so are straight forward on the Garmin 530.

My personal Garmin GPSMAP 196 (Fig. 20) has a terrific feature that allows one to create and modify flight plans right from a special displayed map.

Photo by James Spudich

Fig. 20. The Garmin GPSMAP 196

√ From the main menu page of the Garmin GPSMAP 196, highlight the 'Route' tab and use the arrow keypad to <u>select</u> the desired saved route.
   ■ <u>Select</u> means <u>highlight</u> the desired saved route and <u>press</u> **enter**; this is generally how you select everything on the Garmin.

√ Press **menu** and select 'Edit on Map.'

√ To insert a new waypoint, use the arrow keypad to place the panning pointer on the route leg line near where you want to insert another waypoint.
   ■ The route leg line will appear highlighted when the panning pointer is on it.

√ Press **enter**.
   ■ This creates a "rubber band" line for this leg.

√ Move the panning pointer, dragging the route leg line to the new waypoint that you want to add.

√ Press **enter**.
   ■ Your route now includes the new waypoint. Go ahead and grab the route segment again and press **enter**. Drag it to yet another waypoint and press **enter**. In fact, an easy way to enter a multi-waypoint flight plan from Palo Alto to Montgomery airport in San Diego, for example, is to create a flight plan with just KPAO and KMYF entered. Then use the 'Edit on Map' feature to pull your route leg segment around to select all the waypoints in between Palo Alto and Montgomery field.

√ Edit your flight plan enroute on the Garmin 196.
   ■ While in flight you may want to delete a waypoint because you decided to fly directly to the next one (or were instructed by ATC to do so). Just highlight

the waypoint in the Active Route page, press **menu**, highlight 'Remove Waypoint' and press **enter**. It's done! You can also remove a waypoint while in the 'Edit on Map' mode by just highlighting the waypoint with your panning pointer, then press **menu**, highlight 'Remove' and press **enter**.

A Practice VFR Flight

Let's now return to your downloaded Garmin GNS 530 Simulator from http://www.garmin.com/aviation. Even if you aren't IFR rated, there is a tremendous amount of information available to you via this GPS unit. Since the unit knows via satellites exactly where you are in 3D space at all times, it can tell you nearly everything about your flight. The best way to illustrate some of the essential features of the unit is to practice flying somewhere.

Upon booting up your Garmin 530 Simulator program, the unit will go through a self test and then display a blinking "OK?" in the lower right hand corner. Answer the query by pressing enter (**ENT**). The unit will first show the satellite status page. When the necessary number of satellites has been found, the page will automatically change over to the moving map.

Let's make a VFR flight from Palo Alto airport to Stockton airport:

√ If you are not at KPAO, go there.
- One way is to initialize your position, as described previously (Go to **Options**, **Initialize Position**. Fill in the blanks with "KPAO," by 'rotating' the large and small GPS knobs on the lower right of the screen. Press **ENT** to accept).

√ Use the range (**RNG**) up and down button to get the magnification you want.

■ Start at **150nm-1**, shown on the map on the lower left, and you will have KPAO and KSCK both on the map; try other magnifications to see what you can see. At a map magnification of **15nm-1**, class B and class C airspaces are shown. A heading of 030° and an altitude of 2000 ft will avoid entering these airspaces.

√ Push the heading (**HDG**) button.
   ■ This sets your HSI so you can direct your heading. Below the Garmin simulated screen you have an HSI and an airspeed and altitude control.

√ Grab the right-hand knob on the HSI and drag it to the right or left to set your HSI indicator to 030°.

√ Put in an airspeed of 120 KIAS, or whatever airspeed you prefer.

√ Guide your airplane to KSCK by resetting your HSI indicator to the heading you want.
   ■ While you are flying along, check out your track (**TRK**) and your ground speed (**GS**). Rotate the GPS knobs to see what other information you get as you fly along – to return automatically to the NAV Group, press and hold the clear (**CLR**) button. Use a card such as the one described above under "Getting Started with the Garmin GNS 530 Simulator," which tells what each turn of each GPS knob gets you (Fig. 19). When you get to KSCK, you can magnify your map (try **3.5nm-1**) and now see the runways.

Now that you found your way to Stockton airport, let's fly from there direct to Modesto airport. I described flying direct to any waypoint in the section on "How to Fly Directly to an Airport." But here are some additional pointers:

√ Go to **50nm-1** magnification.
- This gets KMOD on your moving map.

√ Push the small GPS knob.
- This gets the cursor on the screen.

√ Highlight KMOD.
- Move the cursor by rotating the small and large GPS knobs until you highlight KMOD (note that you can highlight either MOD, the VOR, or KMOD, the airport).

√ Push the Direct (**D** with an arrow through it) button.

√ Press **ENT** twice.
- This acknowledges the "activate?" that appears on the screen.

√ Push the **NAV** button.
- This activates the HSI for navigation to KMOD. The **CDI** button must be on "GPS" mode so that your HSI is fully active.

√ Set the HSI to your desired track.
- Set the yellow arrow to your desired track by grabbing the left HSI knob and moving your cursor left or right. If you do not set your HSI to the desired track, a message light will start blinking. Push the message (**MSG**) button. It tells you what course to set the HSI for (if you are near KSCK, it could be for example a setting of 130°). Press the **MSG** button again to continue.

√ Fly the straight line.
- The computer will fly this for you given the settings that you have established. Check out the information available by rotating the GPS knobs.

Flying an IFR Approach

Let's fly an IFR approach using the Garmin GNS 530 Simulator. You are enroute to Modesto from Stockton and decide that you want to return to Stockton airport for the Stockton ILS 29R approach, with vectors from ATC.

√ Highlight KSCK.
  ■ Use the cursor on your moving map.

√ Push the Direct button.

√ Push **ENT** twice.
  ■ A MSG reminds you to set your HSI needle to the required heading.

√ Push the procedures (**PROC**) button.
  ■ This sets up the approach with vectors. "Select Approach" should be highlighted (if not, rotate the large GPS knob to highlight it).

√ Press **ENT**.

√ With "ILS29 approach" highlighted, acknowledge with **ENT**.

√ With "Vectors" highlighted, acknowledge with **ENT**.

√ With "Load" highlighted, press **ENT**.
  ■ This has loaded your approach in the Garmin but has not activated it. Note that a reminder window may appear to indicate that GPS guidance for your selected approach is strictly for monitoring only – to confirm, highlight the "Yes?" and press **ENT**. Remember, holding the **CLR** button takes you directly back to the default NAV with your heading and compass. In the actual airplane you would now fly the vectors to the approach given to you by

Norcal Approach. Slow to your normal approach airspeed (e.g. 100 KIAS).

√ When cleared for the approach, push **PROC**.

√ With "Activate Vectors-to-Final?" highlighted, push **ENT**.
   ■ This activates the approach.

√ Fly the approach.
   ■ You must be on "NAV," not "HDG" at this point. Note that if you haven't selected the correct frequency for the approach, you will get a message telling you to do so. Look for other messages as well. If you have your **CDI** button set to "GPS," for example, you will receive a message telling you to set your **CDI** button to "VLOC," which is the correct setting for an ILS approach. Now here is one of the neatest things. You've reached the runway but need to shoot the missed. Push the **OBS** button and the missed approach is automatically selected. To remember this, think 'the runway is OBScure and I need to shoot the missed.'

Computer mapping systems and associated databases do not provide all of the navigation information needed for you to conduct a safe and legal flight. You must continue to use your paper charts.

My purpose in writing this chapter was to introduce you to GPS navigation and instrumentation. For you to become proficient in its use, you will need to practice a great deal. I hope, however, that this brief description has helped to catalyze your interest in using GPS and has initiated your learning process.

Photo by James Spudich

Photo by James Spudich

The magic of flying is unlike any other experience
known to man

Chapter 7
Tips on How to Remember All Those Rules and Regulations

A surplus of Information

At last glance, my combined book on Federal Aviation Regulations and Airport Information Manual (FAR/AIM) consisted of nearly 1000 pages. Add to this a variety of other books dealing with aeronautical knowledge, and one has a prodigious amount of material to be mastered and remembered. This chapter describes some rules that are frequently misunderstood. The major purpose of this chapter, however, is to encourage you to invent ways to easily remember the rules and regulations as well as tools that will allow you to efficiently refresh your memory about them.

The Requirements for You to Take Passengers Could Surprise You

Do you know the answer to this one? You have three takeoffs and landings to a full stop at night within the last 90 days in a Cessna Skyhawk, but have not flown a Cessna Skylane or Cutlass during this period. Are you able to take passengers flying at night in the Cessna Skylane, a high performance airplane, or the Cutlass, a complex airplane? Yes you are. The Skyhawk, Skylane and Cutlass are all the same category and class, and *the night requirement is three takeoffs and landings to a full stop in the last 90 days in an aircraft of the same category and class.*

What if you have done your three takeoffs and landings in the last 90 days in a twin such as a Duchess, and you haven't done them in any single-engine land airplane during that period? Can you take passengers in a Cessna Skyhawk? No you can't! The three takeoffs and landings *must be done in the category and class of aircraft that you wish to take passengers in.* The Duchess is a different class (multiengine land) than the Skyhawk (single-engine land).

Logging Time
When can you log PIC time?
Would you like to log some time without paying for it? Interested in getting an idea about what instrument flying is all about? Ask one of your instrument-rated friends if she needs a safety pilot to do some instrument approaches. You *do not have to be instrument rated* in order to act as pilot in command (PIC) of an aircraft being flown by an instrument rated pilot flying using a vision restricting device ("flying under the hood") under VFR meteorological conditions.

Your job as safety pilot is just what the name implies – you have to make sure you are not going to collide with another aircraft or any other object while the instrument rated pilot is performing instrument procedures. So your job is to maintain a visual lookout in VFR meteorological conditions, and this makes you a required crew member.

In order for you to be a qualified safety pilot, you must:
- √ have at least *a private pilot certificate*
- √ have *the category and class ratings for the aircraft being flown*
- √ have *a current medical certificate*

Remember that:
- √ category rating refers to airplane versus rotorcraft, glider, lighter-than-air, and powered-lift
- √ class rating refers to single-engine land versus multiengine land, single-engine sea, and multiengine sea

Since you are a required crewmember when the instrument rated pilot is under the hood, you can log that time. Both you and the instrument rated pilot can log PIC time for the time that she is under the hood, but only if:
- √ you and the instrument pilot *agree ahead of time that you are going to be responsible for the operation and safety of the aircraft*
- √ you are *current* (that is, your biennial flight review (BFR) is current and you have all the appropriate endorsements to actually be PIC of that aircraft; for example, see below regarding endorsements for complex or high performance aircraft)

Remember, since you are a required crew member, you can not act as a safety pilot at all if you do not have a current medical certificate.

The above applies to VFR meteorological conditions. Obviously, if you are not in VFR conditions, then you are not a required crew member (you are not maintaining visual lookout!) and you cannot log that time.

If you have been logging any of the above incorrectly, buy yourself some whiteout and go back and fix your logbook. It is now legal to make corrections in your logbook with whiteout. (*Note: there is not total consistency in interpretation of FAA regulations regarding the logging of PIC and SIC time, but the above interpretation is publicly advertised in, for example, the King Schools flight training materials*).

Logging time in complex and high performance airplanes

Speaking of incorrect logging of your time, which planes have you logged in your logbook as "single-engine, complex" time? To log time in an aircraft as "complex" time, that airplane must:
- √ have a controllable propeller
- √ have retractable gear
- √ have wing flaps

Note that a "high performance airplane" is different. A high performance airplane is one that has an engine with more than 200 horsepower. Thus, the Cutlass (C172RG) is a single-engine complex airplane, but it is not a high performance airplane (180 HP only). The Skylane (C182) and the Dakota (PA28-236) are high performance airplanes (230 HP and 235 HP, respectively), but they are not complex (the landing gear is fixed). The Saratoga II (PA-32R-301) is a complex and high performance airplane (300 HP).

FAR regulation part 61.31 specifies that in order to act as PIC in either a complex or a high performance airplane you must have evidence that you received and logged ground and flight training from an authorized flight instructor in that type of airplane. Upon satisfactory completion of instruction, you must have an endorsement in your logbook from the flight instructor certifying that you are proficient to operate the complex or high performance airplane.

How to Remember the Basic VFR Weather Minimums

FAR part 91.155 lists twelve rules for basic VFR weather minimums! How can you remember these? Here's one way to get the big picture.

In controlled airspace below 10,000 feet MSL, where most of the air traffic is, you need good visibility to be safe, and since IFR traffic is being controlled and can be popping in and out of clouds at maximum allowable speed (250 knots) at a given altitude, your horizontal distance from clouds should have more clearance than your vertical distance from clouds. So 1000 ft above clouds, 1000 ft below clouds and 2000 ft horizontal from clouds would seem reasonable. But consider that many times clouds at an airport are at about 1000 ft, so in order to allow most flights to depart VFR, the minimum below clouds was set at 500 ft rather than 1000 ft. All night flying below 10,000 ft MSL, regardless of whether you are in controlled or uncontrolled airspace has the same minimums. Also, C and D airspace has the same minimums. So this part is easy.

Rule 1. Controlled airspace less than 10,000 feet MSL and all night flying less than 10,000 feet MSL:
3 miles visibility, 500 ft below, 1000 above, 2000 horizontal from clouds

Rule 1 is your most common flight situation and so start with that rule. But note that if you are at or above 10,000 feet MSL, *there is no speed limit*! This means that IFR traffic can be coming out of those clouds at a much faster clip. It is reasonable, then, that at or above 10,000 feet MSL the weather minimums for VFR flight are increased to 5 miles visibility and 1000 ft below, 1000 ft above and 1 mile horizontal from clouds. Note that this doesn't apply if you are less than or equal to 1200 feet AGL, since IFR traffic is generally not being controlled in that airspace (see Rule 4 below).

Rule 2. Controlled airspace at or above 10,000 feet MSL and above 1200 feet AGL:
5 miles visibility, 1000 ft below, 1000 above, 1 mile horizontal from clouds

In some parts of the country there is still a considerable amount of airspace between 1200 feet AGL and 10,000 feet MSL that is uncontrolled (that is, IFR traffic is not being controlled there). Therefore, if you are VFR in uncontrolled airspace, you are reasonably safe with lower minimums than those above, so the visibility requirement is reduced to 1 mile.

Rule 3. Uncontrolled airspace above 1200 AGL:
1 mile visibility, 500 ft below, 1000 above, 2000 horizontal from
clouds

But what if you are in uncontrolled airspace fairly close to the ground (that is, at or under 1200 feet AGL)? There aren't many airplanes flying there, and it is perfectly reasonable then to reduce the minimums even further, to simply 1 mile visibility and clear of clouds.

Rule 4. Uncontrolled airspace at or under 1200 feet AGL:
1 mile visibility, clear of clouds

You can remember these four rules by fixing Fig. 21 in your mind (lightest grey, to light grey, to medium grey, to dark grey goes with increasing restrictions).

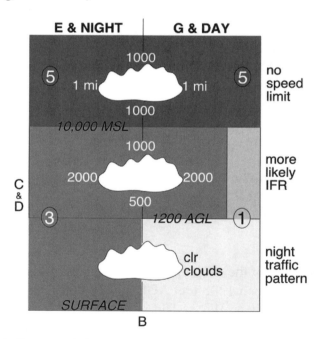

Fig. 21. *A diagram of airspace to remember the four basic rules for VFR weather minimums*

(Not to be used without verification of information from official sources)

Rule 1 (medium grey):
Where most traffic is, from the surface up to 10,000 feet MSL, including C & D airspace –
3 miles visibility/500/1000/2000.

Rule 2 (dark grey):
Airspace at or > 10,000 feet MSL –
5 miles visibility/1000/1000/1 mile.

Rule 3 (light grey):
> 1200 feet AGL in uncontrolled airspace –
1 mile visibility/500/1000/2000.

Rule 4 (lightest grey):
From the surface up to and including 1200 feet AGL in uncontrolled airspace –
1 mile visibility/clear of clouds.

So that's it – four relatively simple and understandable rules to remember. But don't forget that there are two exceptions to the above four rules:

1. In order *to allow one to land at night in less than 3 miles visibility (but at least 1 mile visibility) and simply clear of clouds*, the above numbers do not apply under the following special circumstances:
   √ You are outside of controlled airspace and under 1200 feet AGL, and
   √ You are in an airport traffic pattern and within 1/2 mile from the runway

2. The other major exception is when you are VFR in class B airspace. Since you and everyone else in class B airspace is under strict control by ATC, the weather minimums are reduced to clear of clouds (but you still need 3 miles visibility).

Finally, there is the issue that in some mountainous regions, you can be above 10,000 feet MSL but still under 1200 feet AGL and in uncontrolled airspace – the minimums there are 1 mile visibility/ clear of clouds.

The Flashcard Method for Refreshing Your Memory of All Those Rules and Regulations

The above examples illustrate the complexity of many of the rules and regulations that pilots must contend with. In this last section of the book, I leave you with a suggestion of a good method for refreshing your memory regarding all the facts you need to know.

Remember the days when you used flashcards in school, with questions on one side and answers on the flip side? That method works very well to learn new material and to refresh your memory on what you have learned before. I strongly recommend this approach for mastering and remembering aeronautical facts.

I have assembled an extensive list of questions and answers (more than 250) in the form of flashcards entitled "Biennial Flight Review Flashcards," two examples of which are shown in Fig. 22. As the name implies, these flashcards review FAR rules, issues in AIM, sectional and terminal charts, and other matters that are relevant for your BFR.

"Biennial Flight Review Flashcards" is available for purchase at:

http://www.ajpublicationsca.com.

More examples of these flash cards are shown on the above website. Be sure to check out on the website the examples of flash cards dealing with the sectional and terminal charts. These questions illustrate the maps in color (unlike the one shown on page 125), and questions are posed regarding the wide variety of information displayed on them.

What should your track be when landing to the east at Q68? What traffic pattern should you use? How long is the runway?

- **090°**
  - Note RP 27 means right traffic on 270° and you are landing in the opposite direction

- **Left traffic is standard unless otherwise indicated**

- **3600 feet**

What instruments and equipment are needed for VFR flight when flying within or above the ceiling of class C airspace?

- **A mode C transponder is needed when:**
  - **In class C airspace**
  - **And in all airspace above the ceiling of the class C airspace and within the lateral boundaries, up to 10,000 ft MSL**

Note: Clearly, the transponder must be turned on!

[91.215]

Fig. 22. Two sample flashcards
In the examples shown, the question is shown on the front page and the answer on the back page. All of the map figures in the original flash card set are colored, unlike the figure illustrated on page 125.

(Not to be used without verification of information from official sources)

The modern way to create flashcards is to use your computer and the Microsoft Powerpoint program. Basically, you create "slides" that have questions on them, and then with the flick of a button an answer appears below it, along with a helpful figure if you wish. You can either have the complete answer appear all at once or you can customize your Powerpoint file to bring forth each successive part of the answer by consecutive clicks of your computer button.

There are many great features to using this Powerpoint approach:

√ You can easily modify the "flashcards" without making a whole new card.
√ You can easily duplicate a slide, and thus can modify your question without having to create it again from scratch.
√ You can randomize the slides.
√ You can "hide" slides that you know the answer to. By continually pulling up the questions at random and hiding those you know the answer to, you can narrow down to those few tough questions that you always have trouble with.
√ You can advance the slides manually or set them to appear in a timed fashion automatically, increasing the speed at which they appear as you get better and quicker at answering the questions.

Go ahead and create as many slides as you need to make sure you know the answers to issues such as oxygen requirements at different altitudes, what paperwork you need in the airplane to be legal for flight, when you need to renew your medical certificate, and what the currency requirements are for you to take passengers on a night flight. You will have a lot of slides in the end, but they last forever. And as rules and regulations are changed from year to year, you can modify your slides accordingly.

For those of you who have an IFR rating or higher, you can create Powerpoint "flashcards" that are relevant to those proficiency tests as well.

Final Remarks

We have come to the end of what I wanted to share with you. I know you agree that flying is truly magical. How lucky we are to live in a period of history during which we conquered the skies. If you are like me, none of your ancestors has experienced what it is like to be behind that yoke, leave the restrictive environment of the earth's surface, and be one with your aircraft in the freedom of three dimensional space. In the entire history of man, so very few people have! Once you experience it, you can't imagine never having had the experience.

Loving flying means wanting to master it and learning to be as proficient and as safe as possible. Creating your own charts and checklists on details involved in flying and developing personal ways to master and remember the rules and regulations help to achieve those goals.

Photo by James Spudich

Day becomes night, and you fly on immersed in an unreal, tranquil, almost magical world that you are privileged to have experienced

Glossary of Terms

AD	Airworthiness Directive
ADF	Automatic Direction Finder
AGL	Above Ground Level
AI	Attitude Indicator
AIM	Aeronautical Information Manual
ATC	Air Traffic Control
ATIS	Automatic Terminal Information Service
AUX	Auxiliary
BFR	Biennial Flight Review
BHP	Brake Horse Power
BRG	Bearing
CDI	Course Deviation Indicator
CG	Center of Gravity
CHT	Cylinder Head Temperature
CLR	Clear
COM	Communication
CTD	Cross Track Deviation
DG	Directional Gyro
DME	Distance Measuring Equipment
DTK	Desired Track
EGT	Exhaust Gas Temperature
ELT	Emergency Locator Transmitter
ENT	Enter
FAA	Federal Aviation Administration
FAR	Federal Aviation Regulations
FPL	Flight Plan
ft	feet
GPH	Gallons Per Hour
GPS	Global Positioning System
HDG	Heading
HP	Horse Power
IFR	Instrument Flight Rules
KIAS	Indicated Air Speed in Knots
MC	Magnetic Compass
MHz	Megahertz

min	minutes
MP	Manifold Pressure
mph	miles per hour
MSG	Message
MSL	Mean Sea Level
NAV	Navigation
NDB	Nondirectional Beacon
NRST	Nearest
OBS	Omnidirectional Bearing Selector
PDA	Personal Digital Assistant
PIC	Pilot In Command
POH	Pilot Operating Handbook
PROC	Procedure
RAIM	Receiver Autonomous Integrity Monitoring
RNG	Range
RPM, rpm	revolutions per minute
SIC	Second In Command
STC	Supplemental Type Certificate
TAE	Track Angle Error
TC	Turn Coordinator
TCDS	Type Certificate Data Sheets
TRK	Track
VFR	Visual Flight Rules
VOR	Very high-frequency Omni directional Radio signal
VSI	Vertical Speed Indicator
WAAS	Wide Area Augmentation System
WPT	Waypoint

Additional Reading and Resources

Airplane Flying Handbook, FAA-H-8083-3, U.S. Department of Transportation, Federal Aviation Administration, 1999.

Aircraft Systems - Understanding Your Airplane, David A. Lombardo, TAB books, division of McGraw-Hill, first edition, 1988.

Aircraft Systems - Really Knowing Your Airplane, The Command Decision Series, Volume 3, Richard Taylor, Belvoir Publications, Inc., 1991.

Light Plane Maintenance - Aircraft Engine Operating Guide, Kas Thomas, Belvoir Publications, Inc., revised edition, 1991.

Aircraft Systems for Pilots, Dale De Remer, IAP, Inc., A Hawks Industries Company, revised edition, 1992.

Guide to the Biennial Flight Review, Jackie Spanitz, Aviation Supplies & Academics, Inc., third edition, 2001.

FAR/AIM, U.S. Department of Transportation: From Title 14 of the Code of Federal Regulations (14 CFR), Aviation Supplies & Academics, Inc., Newcastle, WA.

FAA's website (http://av-info.faa.gov) contains a large amount of useful information, much of which is downloadable, such as:
FAA-H-8083-25, Pilot's Handbook of Aeronautical Knowledge
FAA-H-8083-1, Aircraft Weight and Balance Handbook
FAA-H-8083-27, Student Pilot Guide
Federal Aviation Regulations
Airman Knowledge Test Question Banks

AOPA's website (http://www.aopa.org) is filled with useful information about nearly all issues regarding aviation, including weather, the Aeronautical Information Manual, and much more.

King Take-Off Courses and knowledge test courses (http://www.kingschools.com). John and Martha King's learning aids are a must for every general aviation pilot.

The ASA GPS Trainer v.2.0 (written by Global Navigation Services, www.gnsonline.net).

V Flite (http://www.vflite.com) Garmin GPSmap 196 and GNS 530/430 Interactive Guides.

About the Author

James Spudich is a private pilot of thirty years, with an instrument rating and extensive experience in many single-engine land airplanes. His favorite is a Piper Comanche 260C, which he co-owned for many years with two friends at Stanford University. He flies out of Palo Alto Airport.

A Professor of Biochemistry at Stanford University, he has been an educator for more than thirty years. He served as Chairman of two Departments at Stanford and was co-founder and first Director of a bold interdisciplinary Stanford program known as BioX. He is a member of the National Academy of Sciences and has published more than two hundred scientific papers, edited a variety of books, and trained more than fifty students in basic research.